THE ELEVENTH SUMMER

norkus1@verizon.net

THE ELEVENTH SUMMER

A TRUE STORY OF HOW LOVE AND FAITH
CARRY A CHILD THROUGH A SEASON OF TRAGEDY

SARAH NORKUS

Pleasant Word
A Division of WINEPRESS PUBLISHING

© 2006 by Sarah Norkus. All rights reserved.

Pleasant Word (a division of WinePress Publishing, PO Box 428, Enumclaw, WA 98022) functions only as book publisher. As such, the ultimate design, content, editorial accuracy, and views expressed or implied in this work are those of the author.

No part of this publication may be reproduced, stored in a retrieval system or transmitted in any way by any means—electronic, mechanical, photocopy, recording or otherwise—without the prior permission of the copyright holder, except as provided by USA copyright law.

Unless otherwise noted, all Scriptures are taken from the Holy Bible, New International Version, Copyright © 1973, 1978, 1984 by the International Bible Society. Used by permission of Zondervan Publishing House. The "NIV" and "New International Version" trademarks are registered in the United States Patent and Trademark Office by International Bible Society.

Scripture references marked KJV are taken from the King James Version of the Bible.

Scripture references marked NASB are taken from the New American Standard Bible, © 1960, 1963, 1968, 1971, 1972, 1973, 1975, 1977 by The Lockman Foundation. Used by permission.

ISBN 1-4141-0607-6
Library of Congress Catalog Card Number: 2005909266

Disclaimer

Although this is a work of nonfiction some of the names have been changed.

Endorsements

"Writers of good stories provide us with information that draw us into the world of the tale in an emotional as well as an intellectual way. In *The Eleventh Summer*, Sarah Norkus achieves this goal in a sensitive and engaging manner that is an interesting and informing experience for the reader. This story of a girl becoming a young woman while 'growing' through this process with her family, including an alcoholic mother is very moving. I enjoyed it and I hope you will as well."

—Ned Snead
Operational Manager,
Adult Substance Abuse Services
Chesterfield Department of Mental Health Support Services

"Thank you, Sweet Sally, for putting your healed heart on paper from your "Eleventh Summer." You had to grow up way too quickly! As a mother my heart ached for you all the way through your story and I couldn't put it down until I saw how God *"worked all things together for good…"* You not only give children of alcoholics hope, but also develop a candid picture of God's *"amazing grace, how sweet the sound…"*

—Kim Newlan
Founder and President
Sweet Monday®

"An inspiring and real-life demonstration of forgiveness."
—Heidi Wight
Sociologist

"In the many years I have known Sally, I am continually impressed with the miracle of God's healing and grace that is so evident in her life. Her story is a clear testimony of a life transformed by God's love, despite the odds that could have so easily worked against her. To God be the glory!"
—Donna Anderson

"This book is a "must read" for one who has faced or is facing insurmountable difficulties with family problems. Regardless of the obstacles put in one's path, with God's help, an adult or child can move on to have a successful life. The author has not let her past be an excuse for the present. She has used the situations from her past to guide her in making wise decisions."
—Ann M. Lastovica
Ph.D. Educator/Trainer

As I read *The Eleventh Summer* I would frequently find my eyes filling up with tears. How could one little girl endure so much pain and suffering? It was amazing and inspiring that at such a young age, Sally, the daughter of an alcoholic mother had the maturity, talents, and abilities to not only take care of herself, but also take care of her three younger siblings. With some help from her aging housekeeper, Mattie, Sally took on the role of mother. This book shares many heart-wrenching stories of verbal, physical, and sexual abuse that no child should have to experience. Sally's faith in God allowed her to carry her cross patiently and with perfect submission. In the end it will carry her. I feel this book is an inspiration to anyone who is suffering or has suffered from the mistreatment of a substance abusive parent. *The Eleventh Summer* is a GREAT READ!
—Carolyn Carter

After reading *The Eleventh Summer* and asking God to guide my thoughts, these words and phrases came to my mind: *Healing Through Pain, Overcomer, A New Beginning, Awareness, Courage and Hope.* Apostle Paul mentioned in Romans 8:37-38 - *"Yet in all these things we are more than conquerors through Him who loved us. For I am persuaded that neither death nor life, nor angels nor principalities nor powers, nor things present nor things to come, nor height nor depth, nor any other created thing, shall be able to separate us from the love of God which is in Christ Jesus our Lord."* My prayer is that through Sally's story lives will be *saved*. Alcoholics will find the courage through Christ Jesus to *overcome* their dependency on alcohol and their families will be physically and mentally *healed*. Each *new day* will bring a *new beginning,* and they will be *set free* from the bondage of alcohol because of the *hope* they now have in Christ Jesus.

In Christ's Love,

—Sally Rindoks

Contents

Dedication	xiii
Preface	xv
Acknowledgments	xvii
Chapter One: *Grass Clippers and Blue Jays*	19
Chapter Two: *Coffee Colored Skin and a Crooked Smile*	27
Chapter Three: *There Is an Angel Watching Over Me*	33
Chapter Four: *School Days, School Days*.........	43
Chapter Five: *It's After Midnight; All Good Children Are Now Asleep*	47
Chapter Six: *From Small Town Life to the Hall of Fame*	51
Chapter Seven: *Love Is a Many Splintered Thing*	61
Chapter Eight: *The Drowning Pool*	67
Chapter Nine: *God Refines Us Like Gold*	77
Chapter Ten: *The Men in My Life*	87
Chapter Eleven: *Whoever Told You Life Would Be Fair, Lied*	93
Chapter Twelve: *Suicide Is Painless*	101
Chapter Thirteen: *The Angel Watching Over Me Took My Mom to Heaven*	109
Chapter Fourteen: *The Last Goodbye*	117
Epilogue	121

DEDICATION

For my heavenly Father, my earthly father, and Mattie…
because you loved me.
For all children of alcoholics…because I love you.

PREFACE

The purpose for writing my story is to reach out with empathy to anyone who ever suffered abuse at the hand of an alcoholic parent. I want you to know that you are not alone. Although I had no voice when I was a child, I do now. If there is no human presence to encourage or comfort you, God is always there to love you and ease your suffering. I believe all those who read my "coming of age" journey will come away with compassion in their hearts for the children in these circumstances, a sense of pride in their own accomplishments, and the realization that no problem is insurmountable.

The National Association for Children of Alcoholics states there are more than twenty-eight million Americans who are children of alcoholics; nearly eleven million of them are under the age of eighteen. This is a subject that needs addressing and intervention.

One of the worst things a court of law can do is to leave four children in the custody of an alcoholic parent. In the 1960s, the court almost always gave custody to the mother. At the age of eight, my life changed completely when my father left. For two-and-a-half years, I suffered from sporadic abuse as my mother spiraled down into the depths of depression and alcoholism. The months leading up to the summer of 1967 were bad, but they were nothing compared to the torment and heartbreak that would not end until the fall of 1967.

Acknowledgments

I am eternally grateful to my heavenly Father because *with him all things are possible,* and this project from my heart is undeniable proof.

Thank you, Polly Kraus, for being the special instrument God used to convince me that my story is inspirational and will help others.

To my extremely busy professional editors: the staff at Pleasant Word; Ned Snead, Operations Manager, Adult Substance Abuse Services, Chesterfield Department of Mental Heath Social Services; Kit Weigle, retired editor of the Hopewell News; and Harriet Wright, Virginia Commonwealth University English graduate student; thank you for taking time out of your busy schedules to make sure I had an accurate, cohesive, readable book.

My heart is full as I thank my many friends, whom I will not list individually for fear of leaving anyone out, for reading and checking the grammar on many of my drafts. Your helpful comments and suggestions were invaluable.

A tearful thank you to my father, Bob, retired editor of *The Horseman and Fair World,* who passed away just as I finished my manuscript. You were my inspiration and taught me the dignity of writing. I love and miss you.

To my family, a very loving thank you for all your support and willingness to read "just one more draft." I am humbled by your faith in my ability.

The Eleventh Summer

Finally, to my daughter, Leah, whose sweet, heartfelt comment makes me smile whenever it comes to my mind. After reading just a few pages of the first draft you said, "Mom, you're good enough for Oprah!"

CHAPTER 1

Grass Clippers and Blue Jays

During the summer of 1967, when I was eleven, I asked myself the same question so many times it became my mantra: "Why is my mother the way she is?" Was it because she was born in June of 1929, and by October of the same year her wealthy family had lost everything in the stock market crash? Was it because my grandfather deserted my mother when she was three? Maybe it was because my grandmother remarried when my mother was sixteen. You see, I don't really know much about my mother because the only time she talked to me was when she was drunk and then she was incoherent. I could understand a sentence here and there, but most of her words were so badly slurred they were incomprehensible.

That summer, we were living in a small brick rancher with a large bay window in Lexington, Kentucky. I shared a small bedroom with my younger sister, Patty. Sometimes, while trying to understand my mother, I would sit in the middle of my red quilted bedspread, pick at unraveling threads, and try to remember the times when Mom was happy and not drinking. No matter how hard I tried, I couldn't recall even one time when my mother smiled or laughed out loud. And family photos don't count because I had seen her put on a fake smile just as the camera flashed. She must have been happy at some point; I just don't remember.

The Eleventh Summer

As I sat on my bed, one afternoon in 1967, I found myself, again, worrying over my mother like a dog with a bone. So what happened to change her into the bitter ruin she had turned out to be? What made her start drinking? Why couldn't she stop? Looking out my small window I decided to accept the fact that I would never know.

"Sally!"

Nearly jumping out of my skin I looked toward the bedroom door where my mother stood inhaling smoke from the cigarette that never seemed to leave her fingers. Her green eyes were so piercing when they looked at me I always felt like a deer caught in a car's headlights.

"Daydreaming again I see. Well we can't have that, can we? Idle hands are the devil's playground."

With that said, she tossed a pair of grass clippers on the bed.

"Get your lazy behind off that bed and go trim the grass around our sidewalk. And it had better be nice and even" she said as she staggered down the hallway.

I picked up the clippers and slid off my bed. Looking around I found my flip-flops under the bed and slipped them on. I walked down the hallway and out the front door, being very careful not to let it slam. I plopped down on the sidewalk; legs crossed, and started clipping the grass away from the edge.

One of my faults, according to my mother, is that I think too much. Thoughts just seem to always be whirling around my brain like a tornado. Today was no different; I had clipped about a two-foot section when I unconsciously laid the clippers down. The house across the street I was staring at slowly faded from my vision. Past memories took over like a soothing balm on my troubled mind. I could see the house I lived in until I was eight years old only a few miles from where I lived now. It was a small brick Cape Cod with green shutters and a screened-in porch. From the street, large stepping-stones led the way to the front door. Most of the good memories I have of my childhood are from the time I lived in that house.

I can see myself at six years old sitting on the grass next to one of the stones, with the grass clippers in my hand, trimming the grass away from the walkway. I'm a thin child, tall for my age, with reddish-blonde hair, freckles, and eyes like my mother's. I am wearing my favorite pink and yellow striped sleeveless top with matching shorts. The smell of freshly-mowed grass is strong in my nose. My father is near by, pushing the mower over the lawn and sweating in the hot sun. He is a handsome man with red hair, blue eyes, and small laugh lines around his eyes and mouth. I look at him and feel such love for my father it makes my heart hurt. Sometimes I don't understand my mother's behavior toward me, but Daddy always makes things right, so I'm happy. Pulling weeds up by the house are my brother Chip and sister Patty. Chip is five with dark brown hair, blue eyes, and one of the roundest heads I've ever seen. He doesn't now, but back then he looked a lot like the cartoon character, Charlie Brown. Patty, who is three, looks like my mother with reddish brown hair and green eyes. She becomes distracted by a scab on her knee and stops pulling weeds. My one-year-old brother Craig has brown hair and green eyes. I can see him toddling around the screened-in porch with Mom. Across the street, a door slams and I look over my shoulder to see my best friend, Lauren. She waves and asks if I can come over and play. I look up at my dad, pleading with my eyes, and he says I may go as soon as I finish clipping around the stones.

"*Pretty soon,*" *I say as I smile and wave back.*

Suddenly there is a commotion on the right side of the house and our Irish setter, Maggie, comes bounding around the corner with a pair of men's rubber galoshes in her mouth. She is so excited; her red body is vibrating and her tail is wagging back and forth furiously. Right behind her is a man with a very red face, panting hard.

"*Bob, your red dog stole my galoshes again!*" *Says a man with a German accent.*

Dad, trying very hard not to laugh, said, "I'm so sorry Adolph. Maggie, come here girl."

Maggie, deciding she wants to play a game of tag, shakes the shoes and backs up. Dad admonishes her and reaches for the shoes. Maggie takes off across the yard with Dad in hot pursuit. I wave my grass clippers in the air and yell for Maggie to come to me. She makes a sharp turn and heads back toward Adolph Rupp. He almost trips and falls in an effort to grab the shoes. Chip and Patty stop pulling weeds and join in on the fun, waving their arms and chasing Maggie. The front lawn is a scene of complete chaos with Maggie, Chip, Patty, and me having the time of our lives. The screen door slams and Mom is holding Craig in one arm and a doggie treat in the other.

The Eleventh Summer

"Come here, Maggie," Mom says very sweetly.

Smelling the treat, Maggie trots up to Mom and drops the shoes at her feet. Mom tells her she's a good girl and gives her the treat. She gobbles it up and plops down on the porch to rest because she is exhausted from the game. Dad walks over and reaches down to pick up the galoshes. Trying to avoid the dog saliva dripping from them, my father hands the galoshes to Mister Rupp.

"Adolph I really am sorry, she seems to have some uncontrollable shoe fetish. But we are working toward getting her help."

The humor seems lost on Adolph so Dad changes the subject and asks him if he's gearing up for the next basketball season. Mr. Rupp is the basketball coach at the University of Kentucky. This is a subject Adolph enjoys and they continue to talk. I don't understand basketball so I go back to clipping the grass. I giggle as I start to clip thinking about Maggie holding those shoes in her mouth.

This is one of my favorite memories, probably because it was so normal. By the summer of my eleventh year any semblance to a normal existence had disappeared.

My memory moves forward. *It's Christmas. I'm seven, and Santa Claus has given me the very bike I had asked for in the letter I wrote to the North Pole. It's much bigger than my old two-wheeler and is green with silver trim. I can't help but stare at it as I sit on the living room floor opening all my other gifts. I love the sound the wrapping paper makes as we rip it off our presents. Patty and I are in matching pink pajamas and the boys are in cowboy pajamas. My grandmother and her second husband are sitting on the floral couch acting extremely delighted over each item we show to them. Mom is sitting on the brown loveseat with no expression at all on her face, but Daddy is laughing and smiling.*

Suddenly, a bad memory intrudes on my reminiscence. *It is around one in the afternoon of that same Christmas day. The smell of turkey roasting in the oven is heavenly, so I start to enter the kitchen but stop when I hear Grandma and Mom arguing. I know it's impolite to eavesdrop, but I can't help pausing for a minute to peer around the doorjamb and listen. Mom is crying and spilling her drink as she gestures with her hands.*

"You never believe a thing I tell you. You have blamed me for everything that has gone wrong my whole life," my mother says.

Grass Clippers and Blue Jays

Speaking calmly, as if to a child, my grandmother replies, "That's not true, Marianne. You have brought all your problems on yourself with your excessive drinking. Please put that drink down so we can all enjoy the rest of the day together."

Looking at my grandmother with malevolence, she says, "You know what, Mother? Sometimes I really hate you."

I don't wait around to hear anymore, but head out the door to ride my new bike. My boots make a crunching sound as I walk across the snow that fell last night and blessed us with a white Christmas. I lift up my head and let out a breath, watching it rise like smoke into the air. My bike is sitting in the driveway, bright and shiny new.

It is amazing how flying down the street on the best bike in the whole world, with the cold wind rushing in my face, can make me forget the worries in my life.

Around three in the afternoon, we sit down to Christmas dinner. There is tension between Mom and Grandma. Grandma teases us about not wanting to eat the oyster dressing; which I feed to Maggie, our Irish setter, when no one is looking. Mom barely touches her food just moves it back and forth across the plate with her fork. Taking sips of her drink she ignores all of us until there is a breach of etiquette. No napkins on the table, no elbows on the table, and only speak when spoken to. Sometimes it feels more like a military camp than a home. Dad on the other hand is either thoroughly enjoying himself or pretending very well. He asks each of us what we thought about our gifts and did Santa get them right. He has us laughing and enjoying the meal.

It wasn't too long after that Christmas when I realized Santa and his flying reindeer really weren't logical, and I stopped believing. But for that Christmas, I did believe; and the joy of putting decorations on the tree, opening gifts, and eating Christmas dinner with my family is still a fond memory.

Slowly the vision of that Christmas fades away, and it is the next summer. *We are making our annual trek to Pleasant Lake, Wisconsin for summer vacation. This is close to the area where my parents grew up, and various relatives pop in and out during our two months' stay. The cottage we rent is built right on the lake. It is a huge, two-story cedar dwelling with a large screened porch for eating meals and playing card games. I count twenty* wooden steps leading down to the pier. Dad tells me that the winters are so cold here that the pier has to be removed plank by plank and stored. The first thing I do upon arriving is run down on the pier to look at the fish. I find that I am better at looking at them than catching them with a fishing pole. The only time I catch a fish the whole summer is when my pole is dangling in the water with no worm on it. I'm watching my step-grandfather, Volney, pick out a worm when I feel a tug at the end of the pole. Puzzled, I turn around and see the line moving in the water. I jerk the line out of the water and squeak like a mouse when a sunfish flaps in my face. I drop the pole and Volney catches it before it hits the water.

"See," he smiles, "you didn't need me at all."

Our first night there I'm so excited I can't sleep. Patty starts grinding her teeth beside me, so I shake her to make her quit. She also tends to wet the bed, so I scoot as close to the edge as I can. The croaking of a thousand frogs is like a lullaby and I finally fall asleep.

Two of the things I like least about the lake are the snakes and rats, which are far too numerous. The snakes are fairly small, but the rats are the size of a small dog. Once in a while, I would see them dart out from the brush or from under an abandoned rowboat. They give me the creeps with their huge dirty gray bodies and long naked pink tails. And the worst thing I discovered about rats is that they can swim.

One day Chip, Patty, and I are swimming by the pier in our life preservers, while Mom and Craig watch us from the porch. I'm looking toward the shore when I see one of those nasty creatures scurry out from under a boat and slide into the water at the edge of the lake. I start yelling for divine intervention as I kick frantically toward the ladder nailed to the pier. My brother and sister don't see the rat, but because I'm yelling they also start screaming. My parents and everyone within hearing distance run down to the lake to see what's happening.

Breathing heavily as he climbs out of the water, Chip says it was the largest snake he'd ever seen.

Craig, who is almost three, is jumping up and down yelling, "Shark!"

Patty, looking fearfully back at the water, says, "How would you know? You weren't even swimming."

"Because."

And who can argue with that logic? Completely embarrassed by all the commotion we're causing, I admit it was just a rat.

"But, Dad, it had to have been the biggest rat I've ever seen!" I say earnestly.

He gives me a hug and says, "It's okay. They really scare me, too."

On a daily basis, life at the lake is not that dramatic. We eat good food, swim in the lake, hunt for worms to go fishing, and play card games with grandma in the evening. On two occasions Dad takes us all to the Sterlingworth Inn, where he and Mom drink and visit with friends in the basement lounge. My siblings and I like to play with the miniature bowling alley. Of course, they are not too happy as I continue to win each game.

Chip says, "Come on, Sally, let me win one."

Four-year old Patty pipes up, "Yeah, it's no fair if you win all the time."

Laughing, I back off and let him win. I also get to play at being an adult by generously ordering a round of Shirley Temples (Seven-Up and cherry juice) for all of us. The boys start to protest, so I change their orders to Roy Rogers. It's the same drink, but being called a Roy Rogers makes all the difference in the world to the boys.

It's our last day at the lake and I'm packing my suitcase for the trip back to Lexington. I pause to listen to a blue jay calling outside the window. I don't like blue jays; Dad told me they steal other birds' eggs. For some reason, thinking about it makes me very mad, and I shout out the window at the bird until he flies off. My anger isn't really with the bird – I'm just on edge because of my parents. I don't know what it is, but something about my parents has changed. Dad spent one week with us, out of the whole two months, saying he had to work. He and Mom barely said two words to each other the week he joined us. When I pull back from the window, Patty is looking at me like I've lost my mind. The look on her face is so comical I forget my anger and start laughing.

As we leave the driveway, I take one last look at the cottage, and at Grandma and Volney waving at us from the porch. For some reason, I feel very uneasy as we leave my grandparents behind.

Maybe I sensed that the very taut string that was holding our family together was about to snap. It was just two months after that last memory that my Dad moved out of the house and my world fell apart.

The Eleventh Summer

The movie reel of my memories slowly clicked to a halt, and I found myself staring at the neighbors' house across the street. A blue jay call made me jump, and I smiled at the irony. Sighing, I went back to work trimming the grass.

Thirty minutes later, I finished and unfolding my legs, I pushed myself to my feet. I knew Mom would be searching me out soon to criticize my trimming, so trying to avoid her I headed down to the TV room in the basement to find Mattie. Mattie was a blessing sent by God to love and protect four innocent children.

CHAPTER 2

COFFEE COLORED SKIN AND A CROOKED SMILE

I walked around the right side of the house and down the driveway to the garage. The garage/basement was one huge room running the length of the house. The back area of the basement had been converted into a TV room and Mattie's bedroom. As I walked through the garage entrance, I glimpsed Mattie sitting on the end of her bed ironing our clothes. For a few minutes I just stood at the door and took in the wonder that was Mattie.

Mattie came to live with us in the fall of 1963. My dad hired her to be the live-in housekeeper and take care of his four children during the week, because he knew there would be many times Mom would be incapable of even the simple task of bathing us. He had done it on many occasions before the divorce. Trying to describe what Mattie meant to me is impossible, but I can tell who she was and what she did for me.

Mattie loved to tell me the story of when she first saw me on a cold autumn morning in 1963. She walked through the front door, and my brothers, Chip and Craig, and my sister, Patty, all ran to meet her with big hugs. And when I say big hugs, I mean big hugs. Mattie was the color of coffee lightened by a bit of cream. She was a big woman with quite a hefty bosom and generous hips. She had short dark hair with a bit of gray and the most loving brown eyes. When she smiled, as she was doing now, one corner of her mouth crooked higher than the other.

"Where's your older sister?" she asked, looking around the room.

The Eleventh Summer

Patty told her I was in the kitchen. Walking with a slight limp from a fall years before, she went through the dining room into the kitchen. She said she saw a tall, skinny child standing on a stool at the stove, making bacon and eggs for her brothers and sisters so they wouldn't be late for school.

"Honey," Mattie said, "why don't you let me finish those eggs and you can set the table." As I turned and green eyes met brown, something very personal passed between us. It was love at first sight. I had recently turned eight and was not well equipped to suddenly take on the role of mother to three children. My father had moved out the week before, and Mom had been hitting the vodka pretty hard. That was the week I was forced to grow up and leave childhood behind forever. Years later, Mattie told me I was the most mature child she had ever cared for. She was my anchor, my safe haven during the week, just as my father was on the weekends when we were with him.

Mattie was in her sixties and the most devout Christian woman I had ever met. She had worked for many families over the years, and although she had cared for many children, we knew she loved us like her own. She realized immediately after starting her employment with us that the woman she was working for was not capable of being a mother. She said it broke her heart and she took it upon herself to fill that role. She was my mother in all ways except biologically.

At night Mattie would pull her black-rimmed glasses out of the drawer beside her bed and read from the Bible before she went to sleep. When the four of us went to say goodnight, we would ask her to read a story. We would cuddle up as close to Mattie as we could get and she would tell us stories about Noah, Jonah and the whale, David and Goliath, and my personal favorite, Baby Jesus. She also talked about how God loves us and answers all our prayers. The last thing she did was sing a Christian children's song, and we would all join in. Occasionally, she would sing us a pop song that she liked. I can remember only a line of one of my favorites that she taught us: "and they all went to heaven in a little row boat." Years later, in 2003 I heard that song on a television show called "American Dreams." It was the first time I could remember hearing that song since Mattie sang it to us all those years ago.

Coffee Colored Skin and a Crooked Smile

Mattie would also tell me stories of growing up on a farm in North Carolina with two sisters and no brother, because he died as an infant.

"How did he die, Mattie?" I asked.

She told me they were very poor growing up, and every member of the family worked in the fields just to keep food on the table. They couldn't afford a babysitter to watch the baby, so they would put him in the corncrib for safekeeping. One day coming back from the fields, Mattie's mother found the baby dead from suffocation. Some of the corn had come loose, fallen down, and smothered him. Mattie would say it as a matter of fact. These things happen. It is part of God's plan. Sometimes I wondered about a plan that would allow that little baby to die. She would tell me that when I was older, God himself would help me understand His ways (and He has).

One of my favorite stories was the story of Mattie getting married. When she was fifteen, she fell in love with a farmer up the road from her house who had recently lost his wife. The farmer had five children.

"His name was Thomas, not Tom," she told me.

She told her daddy that they were getting married. He was not happy at all because Thomas was many years older, but Mattie didn't care. One day he just showed up in his buckboard and took her with him. They had five more children together and, over the years, I got to meet each one. Sometimes she would take me with her to her daughter Prudella's house and I would play with her kids. They were so friendly and loving to me, I could have stayed forever.

I credit Mattie for teaching me about unconditional love. God gives it to us, but Mattie showed it to me on a tangible level. Everyday, in every way, she was gentle, kind, and nonjudgmental. She would say things like, "You sure would be helping old Mattie out a whole lot if you would set the table." Or "Lord, child, that was the sweetest thing anyone has ever done," when I would bring her the clothes out of the dryer. If Mom was on a rampage about bringing in dirt on my shoes, Mattie would say that it was okay, everyone forgets things now and then.

Mattie also had a wonderful sense of humor. When I was eight, I asked her why she looked different from me. She said we were different colors because God loved variety. Then I asked why her nose and mouth were so big.

The Eleventh Summer

"Well, now," she said, "That's a very funny story. When God was handing out the noses and lips He told all the people He had created to form a single line. The colored folks were lazy and ended up at the end of the line; therefore, they got the leftover noses and lips. And the reason black folks' hair is different from white folks' hair is because we thought we would be clever and get to the hair before anyone else. We pulled the hair off the drying line while it was still wet."

"So what happened next?" I asked eagerly.

Mattie would shrug her shoulders and laugh, saying that the hair never dried right.

Sometimes I would snuggle close to Mattie on her bed as she played solitaire on an old wooden bed board and ask the questions I couldn't ask my mother. It was Mattie who taught me all people are the same in God's eyes, whether black or white, fat or skinny, short or tall. Also, that we were living in a very important time in history as her people fought for civil rights. I knew about Dr. Martin Luther King, Jr., but Mattie helped me understand the passion he had for all people to be equal. I would ask her what she meant by equal. She would explain that white folks and black folks were not allowed to sit together in restaurants and movie theaters.

"Well that's not fair!" I said indignantly.

"And that's part of what the civil rights marches are all about." She replied. Mattie felt that the world would be a better place if we could all just love each other. But how could she possibly love my mother when she was so hateful all the time?

Somehow, she could see straight into my mother's heart, something none of the rest of us could do, and she loved her. Mattie would bathe Mom, feed her, and put her to bed just like a child. Walking by the bathroom one day, I paused to watch Mattie, bent over the tub, bathing my intoxicated mother. Mom looked up into Mattie's caring brown eyes as she was shampooing her thinning hair; and with pure misery in her voice, she said, "You're the only person in the world who loves me."

Mattie just looked at her with her wonderfully kind smile, and said, "That's not true, honey. God loves you always and so do your children."

Coffee Colored Skin and a Crooked Smile

One of the things I loved best about Mattie was that she was always consistent. She knew a set routine would help me feel safe. Five days out of the week I could count on finding Mattie busy ironing our clothes and watching television when I came home from school. I would put my books on the floor and Mattie would give me a big hug and kiss. I would sit beside her and she would ask me about my day and I would ask about her day. She would tell me the iron was giving her fits or the washer was spitting soap. I loved to hear about all her miscellaneous grievances. It felt so normal in an increasing abnormal life. By the end of our first year together we had formed an unbreakable bond. All the empty spaces I had in me, unfilled by my mother's love, Mattie filled to overflowing.

Still standing at the garage entrance, a huge grin spread across my face as I made my way across the floor. Sitting down next to Mattie, I laid my head on her shoulder. She let go of the shirt she was ironing to give me a hug. It occurred to me how grateful I was for every day I had with her, because I knew in a wink of an eye she could disappear from my life as she had the year I turned ten.

CHAPTER 3

There Is an Angel Watching Over Me

In 1965, not long before my tenth birthday, Mom moved us to Milwaukee, Wisconsin, to be near her mother, and Mattie didn't go with us. I was devastated. I also knew I was in serious trouble. With no Mattie around, I would be in charge of my brothers and sister. Dad was furious, but there was nothing he could do. My grandmother promised to check on us every day, and that pacified him a bit. Mom was deteriorating rapidly at this time and was rarely sober. She couldn't hold a job and spent most of her time crying, smoking, and drinking. I was forced into making breakfasts and bag lunches for school. After making dinner for Volney, Grandma would stop by to make sure Mom was remembering to feed us dinner. Grandma tried to keep the arguing down to a minimum for our sake. She was a very elegant lady, tall and thin like myself, and I wanted to be just like her.

We lived in a small second-floor apartment in a three-story brick housing complex. I had never lived in an apartment before and found it to be disconcerting to have so many people around. I knew, with people so close, they were bound to find out about my mother eventually. Then the kids would make fun of my siblings and me. I went out of my way to avoid any contact, except for a quick hello with anyone in the building. But the one place I couldn't avoid contact with others was in the basement. The washers and dryers were down there and that's where I did the laundry when Mom was out of it.

The Eleventh Summer

Walking down the steps to the basement a month after we moved in, I prayed that no one else was doing laundry. Stepping off the last riser I heard a strange thumping sound. If you look to the right as you enter the laundry area you will see pipes snaking their way up the wall and across the ceiling. If you look to the left you'll see nothing but the concrete wall painted white. I was looking neither right or left, I was struck dumb by what I saw straight ahead. Through the glass door of the dryer directly in front of me I could see a kitten going around and around in lazy circles. My brain was trying to process why someone would put a cat in the dryer. Logic finally kicked in and I ran to the dryer and jerked open the door. I pulled out an orange tabby and noticed the pads on his paws were almost melted away. As a general rule I rarely cry. Mom always called me a baby if I cried. But I couldn't help the tears falling. I knew how that kitten felt, helpless, fearful, and in danger. Ridiculously I started crying harder. I realized that that was my whole life in a nutshell. Abruptly the kitten started squirming and twisting to get away so I set him down carefully on the concrete floor. Furiously I looked around the room for the perpetrator of this horrendous prank. Peeking around the corner to the hallway was a round-faced cherub with a head full of blonde curls. He looked about six years old. Digging my fingernails into my palms I asked if the kitten belonged to him and did he put it in the dryer. He bobbed his head yes. Taking control of my temper I walked over to him and explained to him that his kitten could have died in the dryer. I expected him to tear up and tell me he was sorry. Instead, he stuck his tongue out and said he could do what he wanted. Angrily I told him if he did it again I'd spank his butt so hard he wouldn't be able to sit for a week. Shoving his hands into the pockets of his pants he glared at me and left. I looked over at the kitten licking his paws slowly in the corner of the room and decided the laundry could wait, I was too upset. I still had a couple of days until school started.

The elementary school we attended was right across the street. That seemed pretty convenient until the snow fell. I had no idea how harsh Wisconsin winters were. The snow would fall till I thought we would be buried alive all the way to the second floor. The reality was that the snow stayed about knee-deep all winter. If we were lucky, it would get shoveled all the way to school. If not, my brothers and sister and I trudged through it the best we could. Patty had a very hard time. She was six and small for her age. Craig was too young to attend. All of us were sweating bullets by the time we stumbled through the front doors of school.

I didn't think winter would ever end; we even had snow at Easter. Easter was one of my favorite holidays. My siblings and I would hunt for Easter eggs in the house and then dress up in our special clothes and go to church. I knew this Easter would be different. The night before Easter, Grandma brought candy over and hid it in the closet for my mother to put out the next morning. After she left, Mom started drinking heavily. She was always worse around the holidays. This time she didn't even bother to hide the vodka bottle. She set it down on the maple coffee table in front of the beige and green floral couch and pulled a pack of cards out of the drawer in front of her. Great, a solitaire marathon. When she was like this, my siblings and I hid in our rooms not daring to make a sound. Every thirty minutes or so, I would peek into the living room and find her in the same position on the couch playing cards while she chain smoked and continued to get inebriated. By the time I went to bed she was weaving around so badly I knew she would forget about Easter. I couldn't let my siblings miss the Easter-egg hunt so I stayed awake until I couldn't hear any more sounds coming from the living room. I tiptoed in and saw Mom passed out on the couch snoring loudly. At least ten cigarette butts littered the ashtray. I stared at her for a few minutes, sadness and anger overwhelming me. I shook myself, squared my shoulders and headed for the hall closet. First, I made up the Easter baskets with green paper grass, marshmallow eggs, jellybeans, and chocolate bunnies. Then I took what was left and hid them around the apartment. After I was through, I crawled back into bed, said my prayers, and tried to sleep.

Chip, Patty, and Craig were so excited the next morning it brought a lump to my throat to see the effect of my work. I just wanted them to have as normal a childhood as possible despite the dysfunctional chaos that was our life. But it also made me very sad to know we didn't have a mother who cared enough to do that for us.

On a sunny spring day, not long after Easter, I smelled something funny as I climbed the stairs to our apartment. As I came eye level with the bottom of our apartment door I saw smoke seeping out from beneath it. My mother had a bad habit of passing out drunk on the living room couch with a lit cigarette between her dangling fingers. I had put out many of her cigarettes and always feared that one day she would kill us all in a fire.

I dropped my schoolbooks and pushed open the apartment door so hard it slammed against the back wall. The apartment was full of smoke. My eyes started watering, and I was having trouble breathing. Through the fumes, I saw Mom passed out on the floral couch with smoke rising up from the cushions. I ran to the balcony doors and opened them as wide as I could. Taking in a big breath of the fresh air, I turned back to my mother. Shaking her hard, I tried to wake her. I heard one of the kids coming up the stairwell; and knowing it was Chip getting home from school, I shouted at him to stay out.

I was yelling as loud as I could, "Mom get up! The couch is on fire!" She groggily sat up and I pulled her off the couch. She landed in a heap on the floor, coughing. I grabbed the middle cushion and flipped it over. The whole underside was slowly smoldering! If it had been the middle of the night—well, I don't like to think about it. I threw the cushion out on the balcony and realized one of my worse nightmares had almost come true.

All of a sudden I felt a chill come over me and I shouted, "What's wrong with you?" over and over until my voice was hoarse.

Trembling all over, I fell silent and looked at my brothers and sister huddled in the hallway crying. I don't even know where Craig had come from. Mom turned her head to look at me.

With thin wisps of hair falling over her eyes, she started crying and said, "He's married."

"What?" I said.

"Bob's married," She whispered miserably.

Since that is my dad's name I said, "Dad's not married."

"Not your father, Bob Sorenson. We had dinner together last night."

I think she was trying to turn the clock back and had decided to try and find her old boyfriend, only to discover he was happily married. That day, back in that smoked-filled apartment, I tried to calm her and my

There Is an Angel Watching Over Me

brothers and sister the best I could, and wished desperately that Mattie were there. When we lived in Kentucky, Mattie had always watched out for Mom's burning cigarettes. That night I said the same prayer I said every night, "God, please let us move back to Kentucky."

Two months after the burning couch incident, school let out for the summer. Mom announced she was taking us to our cousin's cottage on Christian Lake in Northern Wisconsin. I knew what this meant. She wanted to get away from her mother so she could drink steadily day and night without interference. I was only ten and the thought of having to watch my mother and siblings constantly while we were there tied my stomach up in knots. I prayed for God to intervene, but on a warm day in June we all piled into the station wagon with our luggage and headed north.

The cottage was a rough-cut pine log dwelling with cement holding the planks together. My great-grandmother's brother built the cottage in 1936. It had a main family room, a kitchen, a small bath and sleeping porch. My mom would be sleeping on the double bed in the family room and the four of us would be on the sleeping porch.

As soon as the car crunched to a stop on the gravel drive, I ran down the dirt path to the kitchen door at the back of the cottage. I pulled open the screen door, but the other door was locked. I changed course and went down the steps to the small dock. The lake was spring-fed, about two-hundred-yards long and one-hundred-yards wide. There were pine trees all along the shoreline and blueberry patches everywhere. As I stood by the shore watching the crystal-clear water lapping against the edge of the lake, the apprehension I had been feeling since we had left the apartment got stronger. We were completely isolated with no phone and the neighbors a half-mile away. Because of the near disaster with the couch, I was completely paranoid when Mom smoked, which was all the time. I did not want to be here.

Our vacation got off to a bad start the first day. After unloading the car and finding fishing poles, Chip, Patty, Craig, and I went down to the dock to fish. Patty got in an argument with Craig and pushed him off the pier and onto a rock. I yelled for Mom and jumped down onto the rock. Craig's head was bleeding and he was crying. Mom told me to run and get some ice and a washrag. When I returned, she said Craig had to go to the hospital and I was to stay and watch the rest of the kids. The closest hospital was twenty-five miles away in Iron Mountain, Michigan. As I watched the car backing down the gravel drive, I remembered the last time Mom took Craig to the hospital. One spring day, a few months after the divorce, we came home from church only to discover we were locked out of our house. Mom decided the only way in was to have Craig put his skinny little arm between the window fan and the window frame of the boys' bedroom window. Because the fan was on, I was real apprehensive about this idea. Mom picked Craig up and started to guide his hand through the crack. Mom told him to reach up and flip the fan switch to off, so she could pull the fan out and I could crawl through the window and unlock the front door. I started getting more anxious; his head was so close to the whirling blades. Just as I opened my mouth to say he was too close to the fan, one of the blades caught his ear and nearly chopped half of it off. It was still connected, barely. Blood squirted everywhere. I never knew an ear could bleed that much. Being a nurse, Mom knew what to do. She rushed Craig to the hospital. The doctor sewed his ear back on and you can barely see the scar.

Pushing that horrible memory aside, I took Patty and Chip by their hands and headed for the kitchen door. After a careful exam, the doctor said Craig had a slight concussion and to keep him quiet for a couple of days. Craig was such a trooper, but it was another reminder of our precarious isolation.

The following day wasn't any better, but for a different reason. Around three in the afternoon there was a knock on the kitchen door. I looked through the screen at a stranger dressed in fishing garb. I asked him to wait a minute while I went to get Mom. She was sitting cross-legged on the sofa with a glass of vodka in one hand and flipping through a magazine with the other hand, a cigarette between the first two fingers.

"Who is it?" she said without looking up.

"I don't know, Mom."

Giving me a disgusted look she set her glass on the coffee table and got up to answer the door. No matter what I did, I could never do anything right in her eyes, not even answer the door. I heard the man tell her that the Ambroses said he could use the lake whenever he wanted to come fishing, and was it okay with her.

Inhaling on her cigarette, Mom slowly blew smoke through the screen door. " Fine with me," she said with a funny kind of smile.

She looked over at me standing in the kitchen doorway and told me to find my brothers and sister and go pick lots of blueberries for a pie. I found a big bowl in the kitchen, and the four of us headed out to pick blueberries. We found a nice patch about a quarter of a mile from the cottage. It wasn't the easiest thing to do, with the bees buzzing around my head and red ants biting my ankles, but the blueberries were really good. I would pick a handful and pop a couple in my mouth. The tart, sweet taste burst across my taste buds. We didn't quit until the bowl was full. I don't know how, being quite intoxicated, but Mom managed to put together a pie and bake it.

Around six in the evening, the man came back from fishing and said thank you to Mom. She invited him to stay for dinner, which I didn't like at all. She offered him a glass of vodka and he didn't turn her down. Anytime his glass was empty, she'd fill it back up.

At one point during dinner the stranger looked at me and said, "Why don't you tell me about yourself?"

Before I could open my mouth, Mom drunkenly answered. "I'm sorry. Didn't I tell you? This is Miss High and Mighty, or Miss Know It All, if you prefer."

I concentrated on the peas on my plate and wished myself anywhere but in that cottage. They were both laughing and giggling by the time the last piece of pie was gone. As I took my last bite I felt something like a pebble in my mouth. Feeling around with my tongue, I trapped one of my baby teeth and pulled it out of my mouth with my thumb and finger. It had been wiggly and loose for the last couple of days. Hoping for some kind of truce, I showed my tooth to Mom. Impatiently, she told me I was excused from the table to put my tooth under my pillow for the Tooth Fairy. Well, I hadn't believed in the Tooth Fairy for about two years but money is money.

I didn't really expect Mom to be sober enough to remember my tooth, but waking up early the next morning I discovered a dime under my pillow. I thought if I went to her acting very excited maybe I could get in her good graces. No matter how many times she had been mean and degrading, I knew that one smile, one kind word, might make everything all right. It hadn't happened so far, but hope springs eternal. I crossed the threshold from the sleeping porch into the family room and walked toward the bed. As I moved closer I started to slow down. Something was wrong. There were two heads on the pillows, one belonging to the man from last night. Suddenly, I was very aware of the floorboard under my right foot creaking slightly, as I leaned back on my heel. I didn't understand why the stranger was sleeping with Mom, but now was definitely not the time to find out. Backing away from the bed, I slowly pivoted on my feet and quietly made my way back to the porch. Holding my breath, I slid under the covers, trying not to wake up Patty. Some minutes later, I heard movement coming from the family room. I didn't even know I had been holding my breath until I let it out after I heard the kitchen door open and close.

Later at breakfast, there was no sign of the stranger. Too curious for my own good, I showed Mom my dime and asked her why that man had been sleeping in her bed. Leaning against the counter she exhaled smoke from between her lips, and said I was mistaken, that he had left the night before. I knew better than to pursue it and concentrated on eating my oatmeal instead.

The third day, I rowed my siblings across the lake in the little rowboat I found tied to the dock. The weather was perfect – not too hot – with a mild breeze blowing through the trees. When I bent my head back and looked straight up at the sky, I saw just a few clouds drifting overhead. I can remember the sound of the water gently lapping against the boat and the creak of the oars each time I dipped them in the water. Chip, Patty, and Craig had their hands over the side of the boat trailing their little fingers through the water, as we glided along. The further I drew away from the cottage, the better I felt.

When the boat ground into the dirt on the other side of the lake, I jumped out and pulled it up on shore. The kids jumped out and we set out to explore the shoreline for treasure. I was careful not to let the water slosh onto my Keds, since they were the only shoes I owned that summer besides church shoes and flip-flops. After thirty minutes of exploring the beach, I gave up and decided to explore a little way into the woods. It was quiet as I entered – strangely quiet. Avoiding fallen limbs and rocks, I had walked about twenty feet when I heard a bear growl so close that I almost jumped out of my skin. I thrashed my way back to the beach and yelled for my bothers and sister to get back in the boat. They had heard the bear, too, and were already running full steam toward the boat. Craig was falling behind, so I scooped him up and practically threw him in the boat. Pushing off from shore, I soaked my Keds, and just about capsized all of us. I imaged that bear practically breathing down my neck as I tried to get the oars out of the boat and into the water. Rowing frantically, the four of us looked back fearfully, afraid the bear would burst through the trees and into the lake at any minute.

"Faster, Sally, faster," Patty kept repeating, fear etched into her face.

Arriving at the dock, we shakily climbed out of the boat and huddled together.

Breaking away, Chip ran to the kitchen door and yelled, "Guess what, Mom, we heard a bear!"

"Would the bear have eaten us, Sally?" Patty asked.

Holding her hand as we walked to the kitchen door, I said, "Only me. You're not tasty enough."

That night as I lay in bed on the sleeping porch listening to the jagged concert of frogs and crickets, and watching the fireflies wink at me through the mesh, I worried about what new thing could go wrong tomorrow. Exhausted by my troubled thoughts, I finally fell asleep. Thank the Lord, the next day we packed up and headed back to Milwaukee.

A couple months after we returned from the lake, God answered my most fervent prayer and we moved back to Lexington and into the small brick rancher on Pine Meadow Drive. I could hardly contain my excitement, because I was finally back with Dad and Mattie. Little did I know that not even their love and support could stop the tumultuous events that just seemed to follow one after another during my eleventh summer.

CHAPTER 4

SCHOOL DAYS, SCHOOL DAYS........

The tribulations of my eleventh summer started with an incident on a Friday afternoon in May. It occurred in the old brick elementary school building on the south side of town. The first thing to hit me every morning as I walked through the door of the school was the strong smell of disinfectant. I was sure the janitor here took his job very seriously. I was in the sixth grade and trying to pretend everything was just fine. Children of alcoholics tend to be sunny and outgoing (an act), shy and reclusive, or angry and rebellious. I was putting on the "Act," but found out a few months later I wasn't fooling anybody. Do all children of alcoholics delude themselves into thinking that if you don't talk about it, no one knows the shameful secret hidden at home?

I think teachers have a sixth sense for kids with problems at home. My teacher, Mrs. Chestnut, was a tiny woman with gray hair and black-framed glasses. She was kind and supportive of me, and I liked her a lot. School felt like a safe haven. The other children treated me the same as everyone else. For eight hours a day, minus weekends, I could let the tension ease and laugh at silly jokes and boys trying to flirt with the popular girls.

A few times that year, the school bus would be late picking me up from school. Two of the other students in my class also had to wait, because all three of us lived in the same neighborhood. We would amuse ourselves by playing tag or hide-and-seek in the classroom. One gray day toward the end of May, our school bus was late and the three of us decided to play a game of hide-and-seek. As long as we didn't get too loud, Mrs. Chestnut let us have our fun.

Jenny and George were the other two students waiting along with me. Jenny was plain and boyish looking. She was a loner without any real friends. I tried to befriend her on the bus a few times, but I guess she never felt like talking. Surprisingly, she did like to play tag or hide-and-seek. George, on the other hand, looked a lot like the cartoon character Dennis the Menace and was similarly talkative and funny.

George said he would be "it" first, so Jenny and I ran to hide as he counted to one hundred. Jenny hid under the science table, which was lined with beakers, microscopes, gas burners, and nasty, indescribable things in jars. I, on the other hand, decided I could bend my skinny, five-foot-seven frame into a pretzel and fit under the teacher's desk. Mrs. Chestnut just gave me an indulgent smile as I scampered around her legs. George shouted "one hundred," and made a beeline for the science table. Of course you could tell where we hid, from all the noise we made. He tagged Jenny, and I came out from under Mrs. Chestnut's feet. It was Jenny's turn to be "it" and she started counting. Trying to make my footfall as quiet as possible with my penny loafers, I headed for the coat closet in the corner of the room. Because it was May there weren't any coats to hide behind, but there were a couple of old broken desks lying upside down in the back left corner. To hide, I had to lie on my back and scoot in backwards under the desks, which made my plaid skirt inch up to my thighs. My legs were sticking out, so I pulled my knees up as close to my chest as I could, and lay really still. Despite my being as quiet as possible, Jenny must have heard something because she came straight into the closet. I was trying hard not to sneeze from all of the dust I had kicked up. I could hear her footsteps getting closer and closer, so I shut my eyes and held my breath. I'll never forget what happened next because it was such a complete shock. Jenny had her hand under my skirt, tagging body parts that I knew for sure weren't in the hide-and-seek handbook. I reacted instantly and kicked her hand away. She backed off, and I pushed my way out of the hole. She looked about as shocked as I felt. I instantly put up my wall and went into my

School Days, School Days.........

protective mode. I had become quite efficient at it because of my mother. I pushed her out of my way and ran toward the door.

My teacher looked up as I came running out of the closet, my stomach churning. I felt like I was going to be sick. I almost told her what had happened. Why couldn't I get the words out of my usually talkative mouth? I realized I was too embarrassed and humiliated and decided I didn't want her to know. I didn't want anyone to know. From what I've read, most victims of molestation have similar feelings, along with shame, anger, and fear.

In general, children are more aware of what goes on in the world around them than parents might think. When I was eight, my name was mentioned in the local newspaper for having done the proper thing to resist a kidnapper. I'd wager a guess that most of the kids in my third-grade class knew that if a stranger offered candy from his car, you took off running. The problem here was that, in the 1960s, no one talked about sexual molestation or what to do if it happened to you. I mentioned earlier that Mattie thought I was a fairly mature child, and I was. I knew exactly what Jenny was doing; I just couldn't believe she was doing it. I simply reacted, knocking her hand away and bolting from the closet. I left school that day with a secret I didn't share with anyone until, as an adult, I could come to terms with everything that happened to me that summer.

Going home on that big yellow bus, I sat as close to the driver and as far away from Jenny as possible. I avoided her until school let out in June and didn't think of her at all that summer. It's funny how what begins as a major event in your life really isn't that significant when the "trauma train" starts chugging along.

CHAPTER 5

It's After Midnight; All Good Children Are Now Asleep

As I got off the bus at the corner of my street the same afternoon, my emotions were riding high and crashing into each other. Simultaneously, there was the shock of what had just happened to me at school, the stomach-dropping dread of wondering what condition Mom would be in today, and the joy of seeing Mattie. I just stood there next to the bus stop without moving. Part of me was aware that the clouds had darkened and it looked like it might rain. The wind had picked up and was blowing my strawberry-blonde hair back and forth across my face. Five houses up on the right was the house I existed in. I thought of Mattie and the big bear hug and kisses that were waiting for me. She could always lift my spirits no matter what was happening in my life.

Mattie won out over the other emotions, so I forced my stiff legs into motion and started running up the street. Raindrops started to fall as I cautiously opened the front door and tiptoed in. Not too many people had wall-to-wall carpet back then and I had to make sure the wooden floor didn't squeak. My goal was not to run into my mother; I just could not deal with her today. Sometimes, if I just looked at her wrong I would be punished. I turned right into the living room, walked across the green oval braided rug, and passed the floral couch on the left. The couch had been reupholstered in almost the same colors and pattern as before the fire in Milwaukee. Suddenly, there was a flash of lightning, and I jumped. Already on edge, that just ratcheted up my anxiety another notch. Thunder followed the lightning, as the smell of chicken frying led me through the dining room and into the kitchen. Mattie was standing over the big green electric frying pan and turning the flour-battered chicken in the hot, splattering shortening. She saw me come in and a big grin spread across her almost toothless mouth.

She said, "You get right over here and give your old Mattie a big hug and kiss."

With Mattie's arms around me, all of a sudden the horrible experience at school didn't matter anymore.

It was years later that I came to realize just how much interference Mattie ran between my mother and me. She protected me many times when my mother was in a rage over some insignificant thing I had done, like leaving my schoolbook on the kitchen table. Her punishments were neither logical nor fair, and Mattie helped me avoid many undeserved whippings.

Sometimes, even as a grown adult, I miss Mattie's physical presence so much I want to beg God to let her come back for one day. But her spiritual presence is always with me encouraging me every day of my life. For example, when the little negative mother-voice in my head says I'm too stupid to do something ("What makes you think you could write a book when you barely passed English?"), Mattie's voice always comes to me right after, saying, "Honey, you can do anything you set your mind to." All the positive reinforcement I got from Dad and Mattie was in sharp contrast to the demeaning rhetoric I received from my mother on a daily basis. Did she delight in making my life miserable? Yes, I believed she did.

One of the special ways my mother had of making my life miserable was by waking me up in the middle of the night. She would call my name over and over like a siren song from the living room. I would instantly come up out of a dead sleep in a cold sweat. My heart would start pounding and I would start to shake. I would sit up and push the hair off my face, trying to remember where I was. When she called my name there was no point in pretending I was asleep; I either went into the living room under my own volition or hers.

Mom's waking me up in the middle of the night had become a regular routine, sometimes three times a week. The wee hours of the morning

It's After Midnight; All Good Children Are Now Asleep

was her favorite drinking time, with any other time of day coming in at a close second. During the day, she didn't seem to mind drinking alone, but at night she usually wanted company. Sometimes, she would just go downstairs where Mattie had a bed next to the washer and dryer and sit on the corner of her bed and talk as she drank her vodka.

Most of the time it was Mattie or me forced to be an audience of one to Mom's rambling monologues. The subject matter was mostly taking trips down memory lane when life was good. No dialogue from me required, just nodding at the right places. Except nodding sometimes turned into falling asleep, which generally provoked sarcasm. Remarks like, "Am I keeping you from your beauty sleep?" or, "I'm so sorry, please do nap while I talk." But, when she was really depressed, she talked about killing herself because no one loved her. That really scared me and I would say, "Of course I love you; please don't kill yourself." After thirty minutes or more of Mom's monologue, I just couldn't take anymore and would start crying and tell her I had to go to school the next morning. I can't remember what I said during summer break. After I started crying, one of two things would happen. We were either loud enough to awake Mattie, who would come up from her bedroom downstairs and tell me to go to bed. She would then stay up with my mother, listening to her until she passed out. Or, Mom just got fed up with my ingratitude and, after a few hurtful put-downs, would send me to bed.

I never realized how traumatized I was by these late-night awakenings until the first time my infant daughter woke me in the middle of the night for a feeding. The same horrible feeling – heart pounding, wanting to resist – until I realized it was my daughter and not my mother.

On one bizarre occasion that summer, she woke all four of us early on a Saturday morning and told us to get ready for school. No matter how much we tried to convince her it was Saturday, she didn't believe us. So we got dressed in our school clothes and headed for the bus stop. When we got there, I told my siblings to meet back at the house in a couple of hours because Dad would be coming by to pick us up for our regular weekend visit.

On the same day I was molested by Jenny, my mom woke me up sometime in the middle of the night calling my name. When I entered the living room, I saw her sitting in the middle of the floral couch in red pajamas. Her black hair was shoulder length that summer, with only a couple of gray hairs visible. She had pin-curled a few thin strands to the side of her face. Red was her favorite color and at one time it went very well with her complexion. Red did not go well with the sallow, waxy look her skin had now. Waving a short glass of straight vodka in one hand and a cigarette in the other she asked me, " What took you so long? I must have called your name ten times." Her green eyes had a mean glint to them. It's rare, but once in a while these late night sessions turned into what I called the "I hurt, so you should, too," dialogue. Standing there in front of her, the smell of her cigarette making me nauseous, I had a bad feeling in the pit of my stomach that this would be one of those nights. I said I was sorry for taking so long, and she pointed to the love seat and told me to go sit down. I curled myself into the furthest corner of the love seat and waited. That night the subject was my dad, and what a no-good S.O.B he was. I particularly hated it when she talked about my dad. She knew this and probably picked the subject to get a reaction out of me. I didn't take the bait and just sat there in stony silence. After fifteen minutes of not getting the reaction she wanted, she flicked ashes into her ashtray and told me we were moving. She knew how much I didn't want to move and finally got the reaction she was looking for when I started to cry. Moving meant leaving my Dad and Mattie, and I just couldn't do it again. She told me that I was a whining, sniveling little baby and I needed to grow up. Why she picked that night of all nights to decide to be so cruel, I don't know. Mattie heard me crying and came to my rescue. She was breathing hard from the exertion of climbing the stairs from the basement too fast with her bad ankle.

"Miz Hackett," she said, "you've got to let that child go back to sleep; she has school tomorrow."

Mom looked up at Mattie, and a brief flicker of guilt passed over her face.

"Fine," she whispered. "She doesn't love me anyway."

With a stricken look, Mattie gave me a hug, and I went back to my bedroom. When I laid back down on my bed to go to sleep, I said my prayers again. "Now I lay me down to sleep, I pray the Lord my soul to keep…" I always added an extra line, "Please, God, help my mother. Amen."

CHAPTER 6

From Small Town Life to the Hall of Fame

One of the worst things about that summer was living with my mother. But one of the best things was visiting my dad on the weekends. It was such a huge relief to get away, if only briefly. It was the difference between holding my breath and breathing. Dad was everything Mom was not. He was a loving father with lots of hugs and kisses. He was encouraging, respectful of my feelings, and told me all the time he loved me. Mom touched me only when she felt that I needed to be punished, and never told me she loved me.

Unfortunately, that particular summer we rarely, if ever, got to stay overnight at my dad's place. Dad had moved to a little cottage on a farm right outside of town and there was no room to sleep four kids. Mostly, we saw him only on Saturday afternoons and a few Sundays.

I loved for my Dad to tell me stories about his life. His life was one of those small-town-kid-does-well stories. He grew up in a little town called Whitewater, Wisconsin. It was a college town with beautiful old brick buildings, the type of place where everyone knows everyone else. That's actually where my parents met. My mom's family also lived in Whitewater. Dad and Mom's first date was to my cousin Stephen Ambrose's house, the noted author of historical war novels. Mom and Dad dated for a couple of years and married in 1952.

During Dad's last year in high school, the Japanese bombed Pearl Harbor, Hawaii. America was going to war. He decided his country needed him more than the football team did and enlisted in the Army. He was my grandmother's only son, and I'm sure she wished he hadn't enlisted.

Dad loved horses, so he enlisted into the cavalry. His basic training was at Fort Riley, Kansas. After basic training he was assigned to Officer Candidate School, also at Fort Riley. He graduated as a second lieutenant and has the distinction of being one of the youngest officers in the history of the cavalry.

In 1942, he was sent to Africa to fight the Germans. Dad was a reconnaissance platoon leader, often sent out to scout areas of interest to his commander. His platoon consisted of jeeps and light tanks. I find that ironic – trained on a horse and given a jeep. One day, while leading a reconnaissance mission, he was seriously wounded by shellfire from a German 88MM gun. Dad had horrible wounds on the back of both thighs. The doctors told him the healing process would be painful and long. So, for the next two years he was in and out of hospitals.

Once his wounds had healed sufficiently so that he could walk, the Army sent him to accompany the Hollywood actresses of his day on a war bond tour. After the tour, he took the advice of a good friend and decided to go to college on the G.I. Bill, which offered free education to those who served honorably in the military.

When Dad was medically retired from the Army at the ripe old age of nineteen, he put in his application to some of the most expensive colleges with the best education (it was free, after all). Harvard accepted him, so he packed his belongings and moved to Cambridge, Massachusetts. Next, he had to choose a major and decided on the School of Architecture, because he liked to draw.

Dad had been at Harvard for two years when a friend offered him a job as an office manager for a horse-insuring firm in San Francisco. After thinking about and weighing his options, he decided he wanted his career to be in some way involved with horses. So he packed his bags, said good-bye to Harvard, and headed for San Francisco. He stayed for five years playing polo and dating practically every actress and socialite in the area. Eventually, he'd had enough of the playboy life and decided to take a job as office manager of a horseracing farm in Lexington,

From Small Town Life to the Hall of Fame

Kentucky. He wanted to get back to being around horses. He loved the sights, sounds, and even the smells of a horse farm.

So in 1950, Dad headed back East. This is also the time he met Mom. He went back to Whitewater at Christmas in 1950 to spend time with his mother and sisters and met my mom while caroling on Christmas Eve. They did the long-distance dating dance and he proposed the following Christmas. Dad and Mom married the subsequent June in Whitewater, then moved all of their belongings into a small apartment in Lexington.

Dad probably would have stayed forever at that horse-racing farm, but the owner of the farm stepped in and changed his career path completely. The owner came up to Dad one day and said, "Hey, Bob, didn't you go to Harvard? Do you think you could write an article on the farm for the local newspaper?" Dad, with tongue in cheek, said he figured he knew his way around pen and paper and would give it a try. The newspaper was very impressed with his writing style and asked him to do other articles. Dad discovered that he loved writing. In no time at all, other horseracing enthusiasts were noticing his articles, and he was offered the job of editor of a horseracing magazine in Columbus, Ohio. He decided to take it, and in 1953 my parents moved to Ohio.

Dad loved the challenge of getting the magazine ready to go to press each month, but really missed the vast green pastures of the horse farms in Lexington. Two years after starting the job in Columbus, he was offered the position of editor for *The Horseman and Fair World*, a weekly harness-racing magazine published in Lexington. He was thrilled to be moving back. So he packed up his family and left Columbus in October 1955, two weeks after I was born. Dad stayed with *The Horseman and Fair World* for twenty-five years. He was also president of the Harness Writers Association for a few years. In 1991, he was inducted into the Harness Racing Hall of Fame (Writer's Corner). I am so proud of him. Small-town boy really did do well.

So, it seemed completely natural to me that the farm where I visited Dad my eleventh summer was a horse farm. The owners were affluent, and the few occasions I was in the house, I was in complete awe of the many beautiful antiques. The reason I was in the house at all was because Dad dated the owner's daughter now and then, and I had made friends with her daughter, Adele. She was a cute pixie-type of girl with lots of short brown curls, and we looked a lot like Mutt and Jeff when we hung out together.

Some of my favorite memories, besides spending time with my dad, were playing around the farm with Adele. There was a kidney-shaped pool by my Dad's cottage that we swam in a lot. There was also a barn for the horses with a large hayloft. One Saturday as we arrived at the cottage, Adele met me at the car. Excitement seemed to vibrate through her whole body.

"Sally, come quick!" She said, pulling me toward the horse barn.

The double doors were open, and the smell of manure and horse sweat hit my nostrils like a heady perfume. Still holding my hand, Adele led me to the hayloft and started up the rungs. I started up behind her trying to avoid getting chaff in my eyes, as she moved from one step to the next. She arrived at the top and kicked herself over the edge. As my head cleared the edge of the loft I heard a strange mewing sound.

"What's that?" I asked.

"Come on, I'll show you," Adele exclaimed with a big grin.

Pushing myself over the loft's edge, I scrambled to my feet and followed Adele to the left side of the loft. Buried completely in the hay were three black and white kittens. Dropping to my knees, I dug into the hay and picked one up. He was so tiny, fitting perfectly in the palm of my hand. He didn't like being moved. He started squirming and mewing louder. The mother cat startled me when she jumped through the hayloft window, meowing and rubbing against my thigh. Deciding that the mama cat might turn mean, we carefully laid the kittens back in the hay and returned to the ladder. This was the part I hated most – climbing down the ladder. I waited for Adele to go first, trying not to imagine myself falling quite a few feet to the barn floor. Once she was clear, I lay down on my stomach and inched myself backwards toward the edge of the loft. Dangling my legs over, I felt for the rung of the ladder with the toe of my right tennis shoe. Once I found it, I added the other shoe and breathed a sigh of relief. Wiggling myself slowly over the edge, I carefully descended one rung at a time.

When I hit the barn floor, Adele impatiently said, "It's about time."

"Sorry, I'm not too fond of heights," I replied defensively.

Adele looked at me for a second; then, trying to lighten the mood, said brightly, "Hey, if you want one of the kittens, I can ask my mom."

Thinking of our Irish setter, Jeffrey, back home, I said it probably wouldn't be a good idea.

Heading toward the double doors Adele said, "Yeah, I forgot about Jeffrey."

As we walked together in the hot sun back to Dad's cottage, Adele said we could visit the kittens every Saturday that I came to see Dad. I didn't want to think about climbing down the ladder again, so I changed the subject.

"Hey, let's go chase the chickens."

"Okay, race you!" Adele laughed as she darted ahead of me.

Running after her I thought how great it was to have a good friend who knew nothing about my mother which, unfortunately, held true for only one more week after that visit.

The Saturday after the discovery of the kittens, my mother announced she would be taking us to our dad's. Dread coursed through my whole body. There was a big social going on; Mom knew a lot of the people and someone, who obviously didn't know about her drinking problem, had invited her. She put on a red dress and makeup, and did her hair. She was fairly sober and reeked of breath spray. I sent up a prayer of thanks when we arrived alive and not wrapped around a tree. Adele, my brothers and sister, and I played croquet for a while. I think smashing that ball with a mallet helped get out some of my feelings of aggression. After the croquet game ended, Adele suggested we go swimming. As I walked through the gate to the pool, I noticed Chip peering over the side into the water.

"Hey, what's so fascinating?" I asked as I sauntered up next to him.

"I think I see a quarter on the bottom," he said excitedly.

"Really, well let me check it out for you."

Jumping up as high as I could I grabbed my knees and did a cannonball into the water right next to him. Surfacing, I started laughing at my little brother standing back from the edge of the pool, soaking wet and glaring at me.

"Very, funny! Do that again and I'll tell Dad."

"Tattletale," I replied as I turned and dove to the bottom of the pool to see if there really was a quarter there.

I was the only one of my siblings who could swim, so the other three splashed around in the shallow end of the pool. Adele and I had decided to play a game of Marco Polo in the deep end. Trying to avoid Adele's outstretched hand, I dove to the bottom and kicked my way to the surface a few feet to the left. Coming up quietly, so as to make as little noise as possible, I happened to look up and see Chip on the diving board. Trying to get even with me, he gave a Tarzan yell and did a cannonball off the board – forgetting, of course, that he couldn't swim.

He went under quickly and sank like the proverbial rock. "Cool! One less annoying, irritating younger brother," I thought. Dad obviously didn't share my view and jumped in fully clothed to save Chip. Of course, I really didn't want him to drown. My brothers and sisters were annoying, but I did love them. Dad, on the other hand, didn't look like he had that loving feeling; Chip had ruined his watch. About an hour later, Mom said it was time to go, so we changed into our clothes and said our good-byes.

The trip home was a nightmare. Mom sober and needing a drink was just as bad as Mom smashed. On the way home, one of us made the mistake of commenting on what a fun day it had been. That was the only excuse she needed to fly into a rage about how we weren't suppose to speak unless spoken to. I didn't know if she was talking about in the station wagon, or at the swim party we had just left. I got that sinking feeling in the pit of my stomach and tried to imagine what the punishment would be this time. Craig is the one who remembers what happened when we arrived home.

She drove the car down the driveway to the back of the house and into the garage/basement. We were marched up the garage stairs and through the kitchen to the living room.

"Line up and don't move," she said.

We stood at attention so well that the Army would have recruited us on the spot.

"This is a reminder to never speak unless spoken to first," she screamed.

Then systematically, she went behind each of us, grabbed an arm, and jerked it around and up our back until we screamed and begged her to stop. Craig said that he walked around the house the rest of the day positive his arm was broken.

You never knew what would set her off. Once, while smashed, she tripped on the upturned corner of the braided rug in the dining room and I happened to be in the vicinity.

Blaming me, she yelled, "Your negligence has almost killed me. And that would be the second time you almost killed me since I almost died giving birth to you!"

Then, weaving back and forth and pointing toward the window facing the front of the house, she said, "Get in that corner and don't move a muscle." And, believe me, unless my pants were on fire I wasn't going anywhere.

Oh, how I wished I could live on the farm with my dad and visit my mom only once a week. I would be able to play with Adele and swim in the pool more.

But the main reason was to be with Dad, of course, and the horses. I was absolutely crazy about horses. Most visits, Dad would let us climb up on the fence and feed carrots to the horses. When my dad and mom were still married, they let me take riding lessons, and I missed that so much. Any chance I had, I was on a horse. And there was one horse in particular I desperately wanted to ride that summer.

At the end of the street where I lived with my mother was a pasture with a small dump right in the middle of it. The owner had a chestnut Clydesdale with a white forelock that he used to move the heavy rubbish. I used to stand at the fence and watch that horse, daydreaming about the day I would capture him and race him across the pasture and over the fence. Once we cleared the fence, all my problems would magically disappear and I would be free. My sanity finally fled and I decided to do just that.

Toward the end of June, I came out of my house after lunch and decided I had to get as far away from my mother as possible. She was completely unreasonable! She had made cream cheese and jelly sandwiches, which she knew makes me sick. I sat at the kitchen table staring at the sandwich, hoping it would just disappear into thin air.

"Mom, I'll throw up if I eat it," I said as my stomach started to get unsettled. The smell of the cream cheese was making me nauseous.

"You will eat it or go to your room for the rest of the day," she said, pointing her finger at me for emphasis. I took a tentative bite and gagged immediately.

"You'd better swallow that or go to your room right now."

Suppressing the gag reflex, I swallowed and chased the bite with a gulp of milk. The phone rang, and as Mom turned to the kitchen wall I took one half of my sandwich and hid it in my napkin. Luckily it was someone she had to talk to, so she forgot about eagle eyeing me as I ate. Patty loves cream cheese and took the other half of my sandwich when Mom wasn't looking. Finishing the rest of my lunch, I asked to be excused. She waved me away from the table impatiently as she continued her conversation on the phone.

Standing on the sidewalk in front of the house, I looked to my right and saw the pasture fence at the end of the street. With determination, I headed for the pasture. A light breeze blew a Three Musketeers candy bar wrapper up ahead of me on the sidewalk. Each time I got close enough to step on it, the wind would pick it up and move it another couple of feet. All of a sudden it became important to step on that wrapper, because if I did that meant I would be able to ride the Clydesdale. Running up the sidewalk I was finally able to trap the wrapper just a foot from the fence. Confidence filled my skinny frame as I climbed the black wooden fence and plowed through the long grass. Little burrs in the grass kept clinging to my legs, and every few feet I stopped to brush them off. If I had thought this plan through, I would have worn long pants. The Clydesdale was over by the fence on the left munching grass. I headed in that direction and started slowing down as I got near. He lifted his head and mildly stared at me as he chewed. I pulled up a few blades of grass and offered them to Clyde (my nickname for the horse), and started petting him. He just blew the grass out of my hand and tried to eat my strawberry-blonde hair instead. I let the horse smell me, and he decided I was harmless. I was itching to get up on Clyde's back, but there was a slight problem – how to get up on a horse whose back was taller than my head. I checked out the field, dismissing one idea after another until I saw a tree stump just a few feet away. Grabbing Clyde's forelock I walked him over to the stump. Avoiding the mushrooms, I climbed on the stump and holding on to Clyde's mane launched myself on to his very broad back. At once, my legs stuck out straight to the right and left. His back was a lot broader than I thought. Now that was something I hadn't foreseen; but before I had time to even consider the problem, the owner of the dump saw me atop his horse. He probably came close to a heart attack with lawsuit dancing merrily through his mind. Boy, could that old guy run and yell! As he got closer, I could see that sweat had plastered strands of gray hair to his head, and he had a very red face.

"Young lady," he bellowed. "You come down off that horse this instant!"

I could not believe he was ruining my great adventure! I tried explaining that I took horse-riding lessons and if my Dad were here he would let me ride Clyde. I was such an obedient child most of the time, really! When ordering me down didn't work, the owner changed tactics and told me my dad would punish me for at least a year. Now that was a real possibility. Deciding I had better get off his horse, I turned sideways and slid down the left side of Clyde. The owner caught me on the way down. Turning me around, he said, "Now if you give me your word not to climb my fence again, I won't tell your dad you were trying to steal my horse."

Actually I had changed my mind about jumping the fence and was going to ride him only around the pasture a little. But I didn't think pointing that out was going to make a difference, so I just nodded my head and said, "Yes, sir."

"Go on home now," he said as he hit Clyde on the rump and sent him trotting off.

I trudged back through the grass toward the fence, finally realizing what a stupid idea that was. But like I said before, I was horse crazy. Going to bed that night I knew I was wrong and asked God to forgive me. When I got older, I heard the phrase "temporary insanity" and thought of my misadventure with the Clydesdale.

CHAPTER 7

LOVE IS A MANY SPLINTERED THING

Adele left halfway through the summer to go back to New York City with her mother. I cried so hard knowing it would be a long time before I would see her again. I had so few friends. I really missed my best friend from my early childhood, Lauren. She had been over to our house on Pine Meadows only once since we had moved there. I couldn't allow anyone new to get too close because they would want to come to my house to play and that wasn't possible. No one could know about my mother.

The only other two friends I had that summer were Beth Monroe and Katie Bennett, who both lived on my street. Beth was a year younger and kind of a tomboy like me, with blonde hair and brown eyes. Katie was two years older, tall, and slim with short blonde hair and green eyes. I liked hanging out with Beth the most because she liked to play with Barbie and Ken. It was our favorite pastime during the month of June. We would meet at her house, start setting up our Barbie stuff, and pure imagination would take over. I wasn't conscious of it, but for a rare moment in time I would revert to being a child.

One day Mom left the house fairly early in the morning, which was unusual for her. I wanted so badly to be normal, so I thought I would invite Beth over to play Barbie dolls. I knew for sure Mattie wouldn't care. With Mom gone, I didn't have to make excuses about why she couldn't come over. I slid my feet into flip-flops and walked next door. I rang the doorbell and Mrs. Monroe answered.

"Beth, Sally's here," she called, as she invited me in.

When Beth came out of her bedroom, I asked if she wanted to come over to my house and play Barbies. She stared at me with a quizzical look on her face.

"Are you sure it's okay with your Mom?" she asked.

"Oh sure, she's not even home."

She seemed to relax a bit and said okay, she'd be over in a minute. As I headed back to my house the oddest thought crossed my mind. Why were two tomboys even interested in Barbie dolls?

A few minutes later I heard a knock on the door. Running to the door I opened it and gestured for Beth to come in. Hesitantly, Beth crossed the threshold looking around. Mattie walked through the doorway from the kitchen wiping her hands on a towel. Before she could say anything, I told her this was my friend Beth and we were going to play with our Barbies for just a little while.

She gave me a little worried frown and said, "Okay, but not too long."

She didn't want me to get a whipping if Mom came home and decided to punish me for having someone over without her permission.

Beth, deciding everything looked normal, got out her Barbies and we set everything up on the braided rug in the living room. She had many more Barbie things than I did. She had Barbie's car, for one thing. She also had Ken, which was the best. All I had was one Barbie, the clothes case, clothes, and her accessories. Sometimes I would pretend to be Barbie, doing everything my mom didn't do. Sometimes I was Ken and acted out everything my Dad liked to do. I loved all of my pretend kids. I played games and read to them. We did craft projects and went shopping for new clothes. I used to dream all the time about new clothes.

Mom had been pretty good about buying at least the essentials for us until the year before. When we moved back to Lexington, she couldn't seem to remember anything she should be doing. That's when she started spending most, if not all, of the child support money on booze. It didn't take long for Dad to figure out what she was doing, but by then so much was happening it hit the bottom of the problem list. If we ran out of food, he would bring groceries over. At this point, Dad was completely supporting us – rent, utilities, everything. So, any chance I got to pretend with my Barbies, I did. Most of all, Beth and I laughed a lot. When Mom was home, I didn't laugh.

After an hour I started feeling a little anxious imagining what Mom would say if she caught me playing with the Barbies in her living room, so I lied and told Beth there was a chore I had to do and I would come by her house later. Quickly, I started picking up tiny little high heels, earrings, purses, and other Barbie paraphernalia. As we packed up Barbies' things, I felt the hairs rise on the back of my neck and I just knew I had made a big mistake. I practically pushed Beth out the door and scrambled to store my stuff away in my bedroom before Mom got home. If she caught me, her rage would know no bounds. Sometimes I asked myself where in the world did all that anger toward me come from? Was it because of how hardheaded Mom said I was? Was it because my Dad and I were so close and she hated him now? She was always telling Grandma she hated her. Maybe I was just like Grandma. All I knew is that avoiding her anger was my main goal in life.

Five minutes later I heard the front door open and knew that had been way too close. I was just about to congratulate myself on skating by disaster on the thinnest of ice, when Mom yelled my name.

"Damn," I muttered, and immediately regretted saying it. I was going to hell for sure now.

"Please, God, forgive me! I promise never to say 'damn' again."

Oh, no! I had said it again. "Oops – I'm sorry, God," I said guiltily. Hearing curse words constantly from my mom's mouth was starting to have an effect; I was really going to have to control that.

When I walked into the living room, I could tell she was very hung over from drinking the night before. Her bloodshot eyes pinned me like a bug as she pointed to the braided rug. Following the line of her finger I saw that I had missed picking up one of Barbie's accessories, and guess who stepped on it. I had to be the stupidest girl in the world. I knew better than to risk one of Mom's senseless rages.

"Sally!" she hollered.

Wincing, Mom briefly shut her eyes and rubbed her forehead. You might as well add Sally to all the other curse words in the world, because that's how she said my name.

"How many times have I told you nothing comes in this living room? If it had been a snake, it would have bitten me and I would be dead now!"

Another bad sign, her face had turned red and a vein had popped out on her forehead.

Glaring at me, she pointed to the kitchen and said, "Bring me the wooden spoon –now!"

The wooden spoon was her weapon of choice, but the belt would do in a pinch. Returning with the spoon, I tried to gauge how intoxicated she still was. Sober meant I got a spanking; drunk meant I got a beating. Looking at her weaving just a little, I figured for a mixture of the two: a few direct hits to the butt mingled with some near misses to the legs. Depending on how far she missed, I would be wearing either my pedal pushers or shorts tomorrow.

I handed her the spoon and she told me to bend over the couch. As she started to hit me, I just shut my eyes tight and repeated over and over, "I will not utter a sound," as I squeezed the tears out of my eyes.

I hated that wooden spoon, but I would take that punishment 100 times over the verbal abuse I got on a daily basis. That really wears you down. If someone tells you enough times you'll never amount to anything, you start to wonder if it's true. When I grew up and had my own children, the one thing I made absolutely sure of was that no matter how angry I got, I was never sarcastic, mean spirited, or disrespectful to them. Years later when I was an adult, I came to realize that most of the verbal abuse my mother heaped on me was directly related to her drinking and I forgave her. But back in the summer of 1967, I just thought she hated me.

A few days before the end of June, I was hit with bad news. Beth was moving! I was going to miss her so much. Who would play Barbie dolls with me? Not Katie. She looked at me as if I had lost my ever-loving mind the one time I suggested it. After all, she was thirteen and a teenager. As far as she was concerned, it was way past time to leave behind playing with dolls.

Love Is a Many Splintered Thing

I waved good-bye to Beth and her family as they pulled out of the driveway next door for the last time. Then I went in the house, curled up in a ball on my bed, and cried. People leaving seemed to affect me harder than most things. It was like being abandoned. Mattie heard me sobbing and came into my bedroom. Parking her ample behind on the edge of the bed, she gathered me up in her arms and rocked me against the cushion of her soft bosom.

"Honey, don't you fret. You're going to meet lots of new friends when you go back to school in the fall."

Pushing my face off her bosom, she kissed me on the forehead and said, "Now give your Mattie one great big smile." I smiled, because I loved her so much.

After Mattie left my room, I lay back on my bed staring at the ceiling as the tears dried on my face. After a few minutes, I heard someone crying softly. Curious, I left my bed and walked into the hallway. It was coming from my mother's bedroom. I peeped into her room. She was leaning back against the headboard of her bed and crying out her woes of desperation. Craig hovered near her knee with his little hand outstretched as if to comfort her, but was too afraid to touch her.

"Please don't cry, Mom. I'll be good," he said.

She was not even aware that he was there.

As I stared at the scene in front of me, I was reminded of when Craig was born. *In my mind's eye I can see her staring at my baby brother, Craig, and looking much older than her thirty-one years. The ravages of alcohol are already making inroads on her beautiful face. She is haggard looking with lines etched around her wide, full mouth. Wisps of fine, thin hair frame her face. I'm standing in the doorway holding my father's hand. I look up at him with a question in my eyes. He puts a finger to his lips and nods yes. Slowly, I tiptoe toward the couch to get my first look at my new brother. My mother doesn't look up. Caught in the binding arms of postpartum depression, she doesn't seem to care about any of us. I take my index finger and push it gently into my brother's tiny little fist. He holds my finger tight, and I feel a bond of love for this tiny little creature.* Seven years apart, but both scenes so eerily similar.

Overwhelmed, I turned on my heel and proceeded to hunt down every last liquor bottle in the house. In the kitchen, I pulled the vodka bottle out from under the sink. Opening it, I turned it upside down over the sink and watched the liquid gurgle down the drain. It's hard to describe the feeling I had as I watched the last drops drain away, a kind of fierce joy. Next, I headed to the stereo cabinet in the living room. Behind the records, I found another bottle carefully hidden. Back to the kitchen and more fierce joy. My hunt turned up five bottles in all. The most unusual hiding place was the toilet tank in the bathroom. As I sat on the toilet lid, the last empty bottle in my hand, my exhilaration left me. What had happened to my mother?

Twenty years earlier, when she was eighteen, my mother had been a beautiful woman. She looked like a cross between Sophia Loren and Ingrid Bergman. Her black hair waved to her shoulders, and her green eyes sparkled. She stood about five feet, six inches, with a cute figure and an olive skin tone. That year, she was a senior in high school and dating the captain of the football and basketball teams. In their prom picture she was a vision in white, with the most gentle, loving smile on her face. Her date was very handsome in his white dinner jacket. She must have been very happy once upon a time.

After high school, my mother continued her education, attending three colleges and earning two degrees, one in nursing and the other in elementary education. The only reason I have this much information is because my father gave me my mother's two scrapbooks depicting the years between 1946 and 1950: pieces of crumbling, yellowed paper and faded pictures, barely giving me a glimpse into the story of my mother's life. I have no information about my mother's life before 1946 and no one to ask, because most of the relatives who would have known her are deceased. I believe something devastating must have happened to my mother in those years between the ages of eighteen and thirty-eight.

Rubbing the label on the bottle of vodka with my forefinger I felt bone weary. My mother would never stop drinking. Yes, I had battled the foe, but I had lost. The bottles would be replaced the next day and I would be punished.

CHAPTER 8

The Drowning Pool

For the next few days I was grounded in the house, but the one advantage I had because of Mom's drinking was that she couldn't remember how long she should punish me or why. Because of this advantage I was able to escape to Katie's house within a couple of days. Playing with Katie was a lot different than playing with Beth. They had completely different personalities and interests. Physically they were quite different. Beth was short and Katie was very tall. At five foot seven, I was the tallest girl in my sixth grade class, but Katie beat me by two inches. Katie liked to walk around the neighborhood and check out the boys. She was pretty and confident. Kind people also said I was pretty, but that doesn't matter when you look a lot younger than your age. None of the boys ever glanced my way. Being in your forties and looking younger is great, but looking eight when you're almost twelve is not good. To this day, I can't figure out why Katie let me hang around her and her friends. Some of her friends were boys who treated me like their kid sister. So, with nothing else to do with my time, I hung out with Katie whenever she made herself available.

It soon became obvious Katie wasn't going to be available that often, because her friend Sharon didn't like having an eleven-year-old hanging around. I started getting bored. Since hanging around the house definitely was not an option, I spent a lot of my time just walking around the neighborhood by the horse pastures. Sometimes my brothers and sister and I would take Jeffrey and go down the back road by the pasture where Clyde lived to look for soda bottles. To me there is something so beautiful about an Irish setter running free.

The back roads were the best place to find bottles because that's where the teenagers hung out so they could make out, smoke, and not be seen. They'd drink their sodas and just leave them by the side of the road for us to find. We found a lot of Coke, Orange Crush, and Mountain Dew bottles. Chip usually found the most – he had soda bottle radar. Patty found the least. She was the busiest child you ever saw. Running from one side of the road to the other looking at whatever caught her eye – a butterfly, a Coke bottle cap, grasshoppers, a four-leaf clover (which always turned out to have three leaves). Craig was the clown in the family always doing something to make us laugh, like finding a grasshopper on the road and putting it down Patty's shirt.

Eventually the dirt road would dead-end at a sidewalk next to one of the busiest roads in Lexington. We would pause for a moment watching all the cars whizzing by. Sometimes I would catch the eye of someone going by and wave. When they waved back it made me feel special. If you turned right at the sidewalk there was an old general store where you could trade your soda bottles for candy, soda, or five-cent kites. If I had found enough bottles, my preference was Mountain Dew instead of candy. Today they say, "Doing the Dew," but back then we said, "Ya-hoo, Mountain Dew!" It was the best drink ever made. Coming back from the store we enjoyed our loot and the freedom from the depressing routine at home.

If you went in the opposite direction down our street, eventually you would run into more pastures. I had never before walked far enough in that direction to find the pastures, but on a hot July day I decided exploring new territory might be interesting and headed off down the street. That turned out to be a bad idea. Repercussions from that walk came later in the summer.

It was one of those days when the heat shimmered off the asphalt and made you think of mirages in the desert. By the time I discovered the cornfield, I was perspiring like a boxer waiting for the bell to ring at the end of the 5th round. Across the street from the cornfield were a few houses, but directly in front of it was a vacant lot. What I saw on that

The Drowning Pool

lot was so cool I forgot the heat. There were a few patches of scraggily grass and weeds and the biggest tree I think I had ever seen in my life. But it wasn't the tree that held my attention. It was the swing hanging from one of the biggest branches. It was the best swing I'd ever seen. It was made of thick rope and a wooden seat. I couldn't wait. I ran over and sat down on it. This was no wimpy swing you swung on at the playground. This swing could take me up into the clouds and I would just fly away. I pushed and pushed with my feet until I had enough momentum to take me high enough to start pumping my legs. I pointed my legs as straight as I could get them, then quickly pulled them under the seat to get more lift. As I flew higher and higher, my shoulder-length hair streaming behind me, I felt such exhilaration that a grin split my freckled face from ear to ear. That was one of the best days I had had in a long while, just swinging on that swing and daydreaming. I went home whistling and planning a picnic lunch for the next day when I came back to the lot.

When I arrived at the lot around noon the next day, I was surprised to find it occupied by about ten teenagers. I should have figured that out. After all, someone had to have put up the swing. They ranged in age from about 13 to16. Looking at them from the corner of the vacant lot I could tell these were not good teenagers, but what we called hoodlums back then. There were about six boys and four girls. The boys were dressed in jeans and t-shirts and the girls in shorts and shirts. All of them were smoking and drinking sodas and beer. They looked like the kind of kids who might be involved in petty theft, and I found out the hard way that I was right. So, why didn't I just turn around and get out of there? Two reasons: I was lonely, and I wasn't giving up that swing for anybody.

Shuffling my Keds in the dirt by the curb, I hesitantly asked them if it would be okay if I played on their swing. Most of the teenagers cut their eyes toward a muscular boy whose name I later learned was Danny. He had blonde wavy hair and blue eyes. Staring at me, he took one last pull on his cigarette and flicked it across the lot into the gutter.

"That depends," he said. "Are you cool?"

Roughly translated I knew he was asking if I was a tattletale.

"Very cool," I replied.

"Okay, then, go ahead," he said, waving his beer bottle at me between his thumb and forefinger.

I self-consciously pushed my rear end on to the swing and started to push myself back and forth. I felt like twenty pairs of eyes were glued to me, but when I hooded my eyes and took a quick peek, I found they were ignoring me. Evidently I wasn't as important as I thought I was. Most kids would be bored on a swing after about fifteen minutes, but it was a full hour later that I decided it was time to eat my packed lunch. I've never felt a hunger pang in my life, so time is the guideline I use to know when to eat. Jumping off the swing, I leaned down to pick up the brown paper bag where I had laid it beside the swing. Danny and the other vacant lot kids were already eating under the oak tree. Because they had let me use their swing, I walked over and offered to share my lunch. Munching on some potato chips, Danny told me to sit down and eat my lunch. I opened the bag and pulled out a baloney and cheese sandwich. Next came chips and an apple. Last came the small Tupperware container with my kool-aid. Wiping beer off his mouth, Danny asked where I lived. Telling the truth didn't seem like a good idea, so I lied and named a different street.

"So how old are you?" He then asked.

"Almost twelve in October," I said, trying to sound older.

"Really?" he said sounding surprised. "I took you for nine."

Great, now I was completely humiliated. He asked a few more general questions then leaned over and kissed the girl sitting next to him. I knew my face was going to turn red because I tend to blush easily, so I turned and looked in a different direction. Feeling uncomfortable, I ate quickly and crammed the leftover trash in my bag. Pushing to my feet, I thanked them for the use of their swing and headed home. Walking back down the sidewalk from the direction I had come, and avoiding all the cracks (step on a crack, break your mama's back) I wrestled with the thought of whether I should go back to the lot again. I knew I shouldn't, but I really wanted to swing on that swing. I decided I would just have to go when the vacant lot hoodlums weren't there. Problem solved.

As it turned out, I ran into the teenagers more often then not, and being lonely I would stay. So why did they allow me to stay and hang out? I don't have a clue. They used to tease me a lot and I'll admit I liked the attention. Once in a while they offered me a smoke or a beer. That always made me think of my mom and I just shook my head. They never pushed me to do anything, and soon I felt a kind of camaraderie with them. It never even occurred to me to wonder how I went in one month from playing with Barbie dolls with a ten year old to offers of a smoke and a beer from a fifteen year old. Because I felt so comfortable with the vacant lot kids, I probably would have continued to go there forever if something hadn't happened to scare me so badly I would never go back.

A few days after I found the lot, we got the heaviest rain I had ever seen in my life. It just poured and poured. I saw sheets of water slamming onto the sidewalk as I pressed my face against the bay window. Pulling away from the window, I noticed a smear mark left by my cheek. Quickly, before my mother could see it, I rubbed it off with my hand. Thirty minutes later, the water in the street had risen so high I could barely see the tires on the cars parked by the curb, and water was covering part of the lawns on our side of the street. As I continued to watch out the window, all kinds of interesting things went floating by: lawn chairs, a croquet mallet, a couple of pink flamingos, and a very soggy beagle who made it to safety by climbing the neighbor's hill across the street.

It was a Saturday, and Dad couldn't take us that weekend. I was praying for the rain to stop soon. It would definitely be the pits to be stuck in the house with Mom all day. As I heaved a sigh and turned from the window, the stereo cabinet next to the couch caught my eye. In the last few months the only music Mom played were her favorites. If I heard "To Dream the Impossible Dream" one more time, I was going to dream the possible dream of destroying that record and blaming Jeffrey. It was time for some different music. I went looking for Chip. He could talk Mom into anything. I found him in the basement watching cartoons.

"Hey little brother, do me a favor?" I asked smiling sweetly.

"No," he said automatically.

He always said no first, and then, "Okay, what do you want?" I didn't know why nor had I the inclination to find out. I told him what I wanted and he climbed the stairs to find Mom. I waited downstairs until I heard the opening notes to the Mary Poppins soundtrack float down the garage stairs.

I ran into Chip halfway up the steps and he said, "You owe me."

"Okie dokie," I said winking at him.

Mom had gone back to her room so I had that lovely music all to myself. For the next forty-five minutes or so I transported myself to London, England and the Banks' House. I slurped down delicious medicine that changed colors at a whim, put my clothes away by magic, flew around a room without wings, jumped into a magic painting and rode a carousel horse in a race against real horses. I fed the birds with an old woman in a funny hat, was sucked up a chimney, and danced my heart out on the roofs of London. But my favorite part was flying a kite with both a dad and a mom who loved me. As the last note faded away, the rain stopped. I shook myself, feeling like I had just awakened from a dream – a very good dream, and one that left me with a brief sense of tranquility. I turned off the stereo and put the record away, even though my hands weren't supposed to be within a hundred feet of that cabinet. I went downstairs to the basement, figuring my siblings might want to go walking through the flooded streets with me. All three were still sitting on the blue-and-white-striped couch, watching cartoons. Tom and Jerry was on, so I sat down on the corner of the ottoman for a minute to watch. I loved the way Jerry was always outwitting Tom. Finally, recalling why I was down there, I told the kids to get their swimsuits and we would go wading in the flooded streets.

"Do you think Mom will let us?" Patty asked.

"She's in her bedroom. Just be very quiet and we won't have to ask her," I said, climbing the stairs two at a time.

I looked through every drawer in my bedroom, but couldn't find my swimsuit. Normally very organized and neat, I knelt by the pile of clothes I had dumped on the floor and searched again for my blue bathing suit with the little skirt. It wasn't there. I searched the closet and under my bed again. Patty was sitting on her bed already dressed in her suit, chewing gum, and swinging her legs back and forth. The boys peeked in and I mouthed to them to go out in the front yard and wait. I couldn't delay any longer – the water in the streets was going down fast. I grabbed my white slip and threw it over my head, yanking it down until

The Drowning Pool

it settled close to my knees. I glanced down at my chest and decided I wasn't worried about showing anything; I was a carpenter's dream, "flat as a board." We left with Mom snoring in her bedroom.

The first thing I did when I reached the curb was jump barefoot into the gutter and drench Craig head to toe. He looked at me for a minute with water dripping off his burr haircut; and then smiling his gap-tooth smile, he gave chase. After about five minutes, I let him catch me. Laughing, he used his little hands and feet to try to drench me. Grabbing him around the middle, I turned him upside down.

"No, Sally, please," he laughed, as I brought his head closer to the water.

Suddenly remembering the other two, I looked up and saw Chip and Patty quite a bit ahead of us, kicking up water in the gutter. I put Craig on his feet, and grabbing his hand we hurried to catch up. We continued walking in the gutters on our street and the street behind ours. Jeffrey had the best time barking, getting wet, and then shaking himself all over us. By some miracle, we didn't get pulled off our feet by the current and drown.

Soon I noticed the water starting to recede, so I looked around to see if there was anywhere the water might collect at a deeper level than the street. I knew there was a culvert close by, so we headed off to check it out. Once I found it, I noticed it was a lot bigger up close. Looking through that big concrete cylinder, I saw a drop-off at the other end. The water flowing through made a sound like a waterfall as it dropped into a trench at the opposite side of the culvert. The water in the trench had formed a nice-sized pool. It was flowing through the culvert at a fairly mild rate and I didn't have any problems walking through to the other end. Of course, that would have been a good time to check on my brothers and sister, but I was too fascinated with that pool of water. So like any kid on an adventure, I jumped right in that filthy water, as usual not thinking of the consequences and luckily only sank to my chest. That was pretty cool. I climbed out of the trench, and as I looked back toward my siblings, I noticed Patty had fallen in the rushing water pushing through the culvert and was headed for the drop off. Now I was tall for my age, but Patty at eight was small for her age. I knew this would not be good.

The Eleventh Summer

Chip and Craig were yelling, "Sally, Sally!"

I lunged for her arm, but missed. Patty, like Chip, could not swim; and I knew when she hit the pool, it would be over her head. I headed back in the pool just as she went over the lip of the culvert and sank under the water. The water was so muddy with grit and grime floating everywhere that I couldn't see Patty. That's when I started to panic. Where was she? Frantically I swung my arms in a big circle under the water. It could only have been seconds before something bumped against my hip, but it felt like a lifetime. Reaching down, I felt an arm. I yanked on her arm so hard I'm surprised I didn't pull it off at the shoulder. I could have pulled Clyde out of that trench, my adrenaline was so high. Patty came up sputtering and crying. Holding her close, I whispered, "Thank you, God." Now if I could convince Patty not to tell Mom what happened, I could go to bed that night without having to sleep on my stomach.

Figuring time and a distraction might make Patty forget nearly drowning that day, I decided we should take the long way home and cut across the golf course. And if that didn't work, there was always bribery. The minute I climbed over the fence onto the golf course, I knew I was trespassing again. Thinking about it made me nervous, so I started walking a little faster turning my head from side to side to see if anyone was watching us. Water was dripping off the trees onto our heads as we walked along the fence line. The kids were lagging behind; and as I turned to tell them to hurry up, I noticed off to my left the little creek that ran through the course. Normally it didn't have much water in it, but it was nice and full and I had an idea swimming in it would be great. I really did need a big dose of impulse restraint.

With Patty's experience fresh in my mind, I told her and Craig to sit on the grass. Fortunately, it wasn't deep enough to have to worry whether Chip could swim or not. So grinning at Chip and forgetting all about trespassing, I told him last one in is a rotten egg, and jumped in the creek. It was another one of those brief, truly carefree moments I had that summer. In my mind is a very clear image of Chip and me splashing each other and Craig and Patty laughing on the bank.

The Drowning Pool

Sneaking into our bedrooms when we arrived home, we changed out of our suits or slip in my case, and put on dry clothes. Patty agreed, for a few pieces of candy, not to tattle on me.

When Mom still failed to wake up by four in the afternoon, I decided I had better cook dinner. Mom cooked dinner once a week, on Sundays, if she was sober enough. If not, I tried to put something together, usually sandwiches. Actually, I was glad she was asleep. The Sunday before, she had made meatloaf with a cup of chili powder in it. A couple of weeks before that she cooked us oatmeal with little bugs in it and made us eat it because she couldn't see the bugs.

Before becoming an alcoholic, my mother had been a gourmet cook. When I was younger, I used to watch her make dinner on the occasions she would tolerate me being in the kitchen. I would stand on tiptoes, my chin resting on the counter, and try to understand the cooking process. A few times I asked to help, but I could never quite measure up to her standards.

After about fifteen minutes of my "help," Mom would impatiently tell me, "If you really want to help go set the table for dinner."

Most young girls learn to cook by watching their mothers; I learned from watching Dad and Mattie. There wasn't a whole lot of variety to Mattie's cooking. I think everything was cooked in grease, including the vegetables. Bless her heart, she wasn't the best cook in the world, except for her delicious fried chicken, but at least she always made sure we were fed decent meals. Dad, on the other hand, believed that every meat on God's green earth should be grilled. Grilling is what he did most when we were visiting, except for the few times he bought Kentucky Fried Chicken.

I wasn't going to attempt to fry anything, but I did decide to be brave and try out the grill. I located the charcoal and lighter fluid and headed outside. It was a good thing the rain had stopped, since I had no idea how to cook meat in the oven. The grill was one of those round, black, ball looking things with three legs that I dragged from the garage out onto the driveway. I put the charcoal in the grill and squirted it with lighter fluid, like I had seen Dad do a hundred times. I took one of Mom's matches and struck it on the side of the box, then tossed in the lit match. I was not expecting the whoosh of the flames that almost burned off my eyebrows. Funny, I didn't remember Dad's fire going so high. Now that the fire was going good, I turned back to the kitchen to see what to cook. Once I opened the freezer door, the decision on what to cook became easy. There was one package of pork chops sitting on the ice that had built up on the bottom of the freezer. I couldn't remember the last time Dad grilled pork chops, but how hard could it be? I put the chops under hot running water to thaw and checked the cabinets for side dishes. There was a jar of Mom's favorite – pickled herrings. I was positive no one else on the planet ate them.

Another favorite of Mom's was creamed corn, lots of cans of those. All right, creamed corn it is. On the second shelf above the creamed corn I found a gourmet can of black beans. I'd had baked beans before, but I was sure one bean couldn't be too different from another. Checking the pork chops, I saw that they had turned a nice beige color under the hot water. Turning off the faucet, I peeled the plastic off the top of the package. I knew Dad put spices on his meat, so I turned to the spice rack on the counter and contemplated the choices. I really wasn't sure what spices to use, so I just picked what I liked—garlic salt and onion salt. I grabbed the longest fork I could find and headed outside. The coals were a nice orange. Perfect! I can't tell you how long I cooked those chops, I'm sure not nearly long enough. I had no idea pork had to be cooked till no pink showed. It must have been God who saved us from trichinosis. After dinner I went back outside to check on the grill. The charcoal had turned a white ash color, but the grill was still hot, so I decided not to bring it back in the garage. If it fell over, it could burn down the house; and with my Mom's cigarettes a real possibility in that area, I didn't need another.

CHAPTER 9

GOD REFINES US LIKE GOLD

The next day was Sunday, and Mom was sober enough to take us to church. We attended Crestwood Christian, the church my parents helped to start. Whenever I walked through the door, my problems seemed to melt away. All the smells were familiar, and the adults always made me feel so comfortable being there. But most importantly I felt God's presence and love.

For whatever reason, going to church was still important to Mom. Although we didn't go on a regular basis, we were still there quite a few times that summer. A couple of months earlier, I had expressed my desire to our minister to be baptized. He told me I would have to attend classes every Sunday evening for about six weeks to make sure I understood the meaning of baptism. This is something I wanted very, very badly. I'm not sure I even knew why it was so important, just that the feeling inside was so strong to be baptized.

Minister Lollis talked to my mother, and she managed to get me to the classes every Sunday evening. So on a sultry day toward the end of June, I was baptized. There was no air conditioning and everyone was fanning themselves with the bulletins. I still remember the pretty yellow dress I wore and the embarrassment I felt when it floated to the top of the water as I entered the baptistery. I would push it down and it would float back up. Minister Lollis, with an understanding smile on his face, mouthed, "It's okay," and I relaxed.

The Eleventh Summer

I looked to my left over the splashguard and saw both my parents on the first row with my siblings between them. Dad was perspiring and beaming; Mom's hands were shaking badly. I looked back at the minister and he asked me the most important question I will ever be asked, "Do you believe Jesus Christ to be the Son of God?" I said "yes" and he dunked me under the water. (Because I was no longer a child, I didn't hold my nose.) I came up out of the water smiling and everyone clapped. The minister helped me out of the tank and I went to a back room to put on dry clothes.

After changing into another dress, I walked up to the pulpit, and Minister Lollis handed me a little brown Bible with my name and the year written on the inside leaf. I ran my hand over it lovingly as I walked to the pew and sat next to Dad.

I was grief-stricken when I lost that Bible during the turmoil of the summer of 67. Then in the summer of 2004, a miracle happened. After being missing for almost forty years, my little brown Bible turned up in my father's house in Arizona. While packing up Dad's house for his move to South Carolina, Chip discovered it on the top shelf of the bookcase in the den, covered with dust and cobwebs. I told my father about finding the Bible, and he said he couldn't remember ever having seen it. It was just too much of a coincidence to believe that God's hand wasn't involved in that find. So many of those books were just pulled off the shelves and thrown in boxes for the White Elephant store. I have always believed that God has been right here with me as I write my testimony, giving me encouragement in many ways, like the discovery of a long-lost precious Bible.

Another feeling I had besides joy after my baptism was relief. I would no longer have to ride in the car with my mother in the evenings. Although driving with Mom at any time was bad, the evenings were worse. That's when she was really intoxicated, and I didn't want to be in a car with her if there were any way to avoid it. Unfortunately, because of my baptism classes, I couldn't. I usually arrived scared half out of my wits and shaking.

I started having nightmares about her driving when I was nine. The one that terrified me the most invaded my dreams in the summer of 1967. The dream starts out with our paneled station wagon careening backwards down a dark highway. I'm looking out the front passenger window, watching the dim shapes of trees whizzing by. It hasn't occurred to me to wonder why we're going backwards.

When I look over toward my mother, she's grinning at me and saying, "Isn't this fun!"

To my horror I notice her hands aren't on the wheel.

"Grab the wheel, Mom," I yell.

But when she goes to grab it, it disappears. I look at her in horror, but she just laughs her drunken laugh.

"The brakes, Mom, slam on the brakes!"

She hits the brakes with both feet and the car starts to slow down. My heart stops pounding like a trip hammer and I take my white knuckled grip off the dashboard. I look out the window and the trees are no longer whizzing by. The car slows to a crawl and I turn to check on my brothers and sister in the back seat. All three have identical expressions of terror stamped on their faces. I feel a strange sensation, and looking past their heads I notice that the left side of the car is lower than the right side. The car is slipping sideways and down. It's too dark to see, but it feels like we're falling into a ditch. I grab the dash again and wait to hit bottom, but there is no bottom. We keep falling farther and faster. Everyone is screaming and terror fills my mind. I wake up sweating and shaking, the sheets clenched in my hands.

Like a lot of dreams, that one was based partially on fact. An accident similar to the one in my nightmare happened when my mother decided to take us to the drive-in movies.

Not long after the great flood, Mom announced she was taking us to see an Elvis Presley film at the drive-in. I couldn't believe it. She hadn't taken us to a movie since the divorce. She told us to get our pajamas on and she would make popcorn. She seemed sober, but I still had qualms about riding in the car. However, the prospect of seeing a movie was just too alluring to pass up. The four of us grabbed blankets and pillows and piled into the back of our station wagon. I remember the splashing sound the tires made as they hit the mud puddles on the dirt road that led into the drive-in theater. As we drove slowly by the recreation area, I saw kids laughing and swinging on the swing set. Through the open windows of the car I could smell buttered popcorn. Our popcorn didn't smell as heavenly. We pulled into an empty spot, and Mom rolled down her window to grab the speaker box. Rolling the window halfway up, she clipped the speaker to it. We jostled for space in the rear of the station wagon, arguing about whose pillow was whose until Mom told us to quiet down or she would take us home. The previews came on first, followed by the dancing hot dogs and Cokes to promote the concession stand. Finally, the movie started. The four of us had a good time watching the movie and eating popcorn. What we didn't know was that Mom spent the whole time drinking Vodka out of a quart-sized bottle. After the movie was over, Mom turned the key in the ignition and started the car. I didn't notice that she was drunk until we pulled out of the parking space, and the still-attached speaker box ripped the window out of the car door.

"O, God, please help us," I prayed fervently.

Mom weaved the car through the front gate of the theater, barely missing the ticket booth. We were on the dirt road again, headed for the main road, at night with bad lighting, and an intoxicated driver. This did not bode well for my siblings and me. As we came close to the main road, Mom wove to the right and our car went head first into a ditch, three quarters of the car disappearing before we hit bottom. Because we were going at a slow speed, I wasn't badly hurt when I was thrown into the dashboard from the front passenger seat. My brothers and sister had tumbled to the floor of the back seat, also not injured. I think Mom had bruised ribs from the steering wheel. People jumped out of their cars and rushed to help. Mom's door was the only one that would open, so my brothers and sister and I rolled down our windows and people helped us out. I was a little dazed as someone pulled me out of the car and helped me up the side of the ditch. It sounded to me like twenty people all got together to sing a special chorus of, "Are you okay?" The ticket lady called a tow truck and a nice man with two children offered to stay with us until the truck arrived. He told us funny stories to help take our mind off the accident. It seemed like forever, but the tow truck arrived and pulled our car out of the ditch. Relief poured through my body when the driver didn't unhook our car and we got to ride back home in a taxi.

Every time my siblings and I were in the car with Mom, there was a near miss with another car or things not in motion, like a tree. She would slowly drift into the lane of oncoming traffic causing the other drivers to swerve out of the way to avoid hitting her. She wasn't aware of it, but every time she drove the car she played a deadly game of chicken with the drivers in the opposite lane. At least ten times that summer she hung two tires off the edge of our creek bridge a few blocks from the house. I think that scared me the most. Up until July, she had to have been the luckiest drunk ever to avoid a major accident. But then her luck ran out; and my brother came so close to dying I don't like to think about it.

If Mom was going to the grocery or drugstore, Chip was the child who accompanied her most of the time. He seemed to hang around the house more than the rest of us. He was always glued to the television. I suppose that was his personal escape route. I didn't know her reasoning for wanting Chip; I was just grateful it wasn't me. On the rare occasions when she came looking for me, I hid until she ran out of patience and went to find Chip or went alone.

One late afternoon in July, I heard the car start up in the garage and head up the driveway. Looking out of the picture window in the living room, I saw Mom and Chip driving down the street in our station wagon. I'm not sure where they were going that day, but I think it was the grocery store. The next thing I knew, the police had brought both of them home very dazed and bleeding. One policeman was holding Mom up as she stumbled into the house. She could barely walk and had a gash on her forehead and marks on her arms and legs. The other officer had an arm around Chip, who was crying, with a bump on his head and a bleeding lip. The officers sat both of them down on the couch. Frightened, I could feel my heart pounding really hard in my chest like it was trying to escape through my rib cage. Mattie came out of the kitchen with the phone number to my Dad's office. One of the officers asked politely if he could use the phone in the kitchen, and Mattie replied, "Yes, sir," showed him the way.

The other officer asked me if I could get him a warm, soapy wash rag. After the officer wiped away the blood, I could see that Mom and Chip's injuries weren't as bad as I thought. My heart stopped trying to escape my chest, and I relaxed my grip from the back of the love seat. My Dad arrived looking very concerned and immediately went to Chip to check out his injuries. Patty and Craig came through the door looking very scared. Someone in the neighborhood had told them about the police car in our driveway. They both started crying, and Dad told me to take them down to the TV room and stay with them. I didn't find out the details of that day until I was much older. Apparently, Mom had veered off the road, slamming into a concrete culvert. The police officer said it was a miracle that both of them were alive and had only minor injuries. I don't know if they had been invented yet, but our station wagon didn't have seat belts. Mom was charged with reckless driving and child endangerment.

Meanwhile down in the TV room, Craig and Patty were still crying and I was doing my best to calm them. I was nowhere near calm myself, but I put on a good show, telling them Mom and Chip would be just fine. Suddenly, it hit me that I could have been the one in the car and I started to tremble. Chip had almost died, and the weight of that thought made my knees collapse. I sat down on the floor where I had been standing and closed my eyes. Helplessness soon changed to anger and I made a vow Chip was never getting in the car with Mom drunk again. None of us were. After what seemed an eternity, Dad descended the stairs and gathered us together on the couch. He said that Mom and Chip would recover in no time at all and be just fine. Giving Craig and Patty a kiss and hug he said he had to go.

"Sally, honey, why don't you walk with me to the car."

He started talking as we climbed the driveway to his convertible and I realized he must have read my mind.

" Sally," he said very seriously, "you are to make sure you and the other kids never ride anywhere with your mom again."

"Do you understand?"

"Yes, sir," I replied, looking into blue eyes filled with fear for our safety.

"Also, if you can, hide the car keys when it looks like your Mom shouldn't be driving."

"I will, Dad, you can count on me."

Pausing for a moment, he smiled and said, "I'm so proud of you. Mattie's been telling me what a wonderful help you've been to her and your brothers and sister."

I felt ten feet high. My father's praise always did that for me.

"Your mom and Chip will be fine. They just have to rest for a couple of days. I'll see you on Saturday," he said as he hugged me and opened his car door.

Amazingly, through the rest of the summer my mother always thought she misplaced the car keys when she couldn't find them, except once.

She caught me trying to hide them and screamed, "You'd better give me the f...ing keys if you know what's good for you."

I handed them over, because otherwise I was in for a serious beating or my very favorite, the emotional mind game. In the back of my mind was what she did to us the Christmas before.

After drinking heavily a few days before Christmas, Mom called all four of us into the living room. She was standing by the stereo wearing red slacks and a white shirt. Her shirt was wrinkled and buttoned wrong, the left side hanging over the waist of her pants the right side tucked in. Her black hair was pulled back haphazardly with two barrettes. She had attempted to put on make-up, but that hadn't worked out too well. She had black rings around her eyes like a raccoon, and vivid red slashes across both cheeks and her lips. But as comical as that should have been, the look on her face filled me with dread to my very core. I dropped my gaze to the burning cigarette in her right hand, and watched ashes drift lazily to the edge of the braided rug.

In a voice barely coherent she told us we were the most unappreciative, lazy children ever born and she was giving our presents away to the juvenile home. We all cried and pleaded with her not to, but she was getting some grim satisfaction from torturing us. For the next thirty minutes she told us how rotten and undeserving we were.

"You are very ungrateful children. You never listen to me or do anything I ask you to do."

Pausing, she took a drag on her cigarette followed by a dry, hacking cough. Taking a deep breath, she wet her lips and continued.

"Damn it, I can't imagine why I ever wanted children. Children are supposed to be a blessing, and you four are far from it. Look at this living room!"

Our four sets of eyes cut in different directions taking in every aspect of the immaculate room.

"It's filthy! Why? Because you do not care whether you live in a pigsty or not. You do not appreciate the fact that I put a roof over your heads and food in your mouths."

It would have been a huge mistake to pipe in about now and remind her that Dad put the roof over our heads and food in our mouths, so I did the smart thing and kept my mouth shut.

"You leave your toys everywhere for me to trip over, and messes in the kitchen and bathroom for me to clean up."

None of what she said was true. How could she lie like that? Watching her stagger around the living room, listening to her ranting, raving, and demeaning my very existence, I began to get depressed and think that maybe she was right; maybe I was worthless. But then I would remember Mattie telling me to be strong and not believe the lies, and I would tune out her voice.

Eventually Mom tired of the torture, and leaning on the stereo cabinet for support, told us if we scrubbed the house from top to bottom, we could keep our gifts. We tore through that house like Mr. Clean himself, sobbing the whole time. Three days later our presents were under the Christmas tree; but the pleasure of opening them was gone, at least for me. I watched Mom warily until noon, when Dad picked us up for our real Christmas celebration.

The one good thing that came from the car accident that involved Chip was that it was a wake-up call to my father. My mother was on serious self-destruct and something had to be done to stop her. Dad got together with the county judge who was a friend of his and they both decided to take action as soon as possible. The best thing to do would be to have her committed to a hospital and dry her out. They didn't call it rehab. They just took you off the booze and waited for you to be able to function without it. They were thinking very optimistically that three months ought to do it. There were legal steps that had to be followed and a bed had to be made available at the hospital. The judge said if they really pushed, they could have her committed in a couple of months. In August they started the commitment process, and my "trauma train" started to pick up speed.

CHAPTER 10

The Men in My Life

Not too long after my brother's accident, new neighbors moved into Beth's old house. From the bay window I watched the moving van pull up next to the curb in front of their house. Five minutes after the van arrived, a new model Buick pulled into the driveway. I watched as a man, a woman, and two teenaged boys got out of the car. Both of the boys were blonde, one taller than the other. I spent most of the afternoon at the window, chewing my Double Bubble gum and watching the move. Whenever the boys looked in my direction I would duck behind the love seat. The more I stared, the more I realized that one of the brothers was really very cute. I think my very first crush started that day.

I wanted to go over and say hello, and then again I didn't. I kept thinking, *should I or shouldn't I?* The nervous anticipation was like hundreds of little butterflies in my stomach, all fluttering at the same time. I finally talked myself into going next door, reminding myself it was the neighborly thing to do. I ran to my bedroom and looked critically at myself in the mirror over the dresser. I wore my strawberry-blonde hair with a part on the right side. It was so heavy and thick, I always had to have a barrette in so it wouldn't fall in my face. I didn't like the barrette I had in so I pulled it out, combed my hair, and put in a different one. Looking at my face, I wondered if he liked freckles. Enough stalling. I practiced a smile and left my bedroom. I walked out the front door casually, like I had no idea anything was going on and then tripped on the rolled-up newspaper on the sidewalk. Catching myself before I took a tumble, I pushed hair out of my face and waved, "Hi." "Great first impression, Sally," I whispered disgustedly to myself. They half-heartedly waved back, their concentration was on a basketball goal making it's way down the driveway.

I walked across our driveway to the edge of their yard and said, "So, are you moving in?"

The minute I said it, I wanted to take it back. Twin pairs of blue eyes said what I was thinking, "Isn't that obvious?" To cover my embarrassment I jumped in with all kinds of questions. I found out they were thirteen-year-old fraternal twins. Their names were Pat and Matt. They had just arrived from Paris, France, where their dad had been stationed with the military. They didn't know how long they would be living in Lexington.

After about ten minutes of patiently answering the questions of an annoying eleven-year-old girl, they looked at each other and said it was nice to meet me, but they had to help with the unpacking. As they turned to go, I stared at Pat's back – the one I thought was cute – with a dreamy look on my face. Finally coming out of my trance a few minutes later, I realized I was standing at the edge of their yard staring at nothing. Okay, another embarrassing moment; I really needed to get a grip. As I started down the driveway to the back of the house, I started formulating a plan to get Pat to like me. First crushes are so special; all about hopes, dreams, and the possibilities of everything.

For the next month, anytime I saw Pat outside playing basketball, I would nonchalantly take out the garbage, which, of course, was my brother Chip's job. While dumping the kitchen garbage into the trashcan, I would casually look over at Pat and say, "Hi." He would wave or say "Hey" and go right back to shooting hoops.

Meanwhile, Chip thought I had lost my mind. After the third time I had taken his garbage out, he asked me why I was doing it.

"Well," I responded, "I just loved my brother so much I wanted to give him a break."

His blue eyes lit up and he laughed out loud; "Oh, that's a good one," he said.

The Men in My Life

I quickly put my hand over his mouth and shook my head no. The last thing we needed was Mom coming into the kitchen wanting to know what was so funny. Humor did not amuse her.

Because of Pat, Katie and I now had something in common – boys we had crushes on. I started spending more time with her and her friends, watching how the girls were interacting with the boys. I was learning how to flirt. Watching Katie and Sharon, flirting seemed mostly to consist of laughing at bad jokes, opening your eyes very wide and throwing your hair around. Well to be honest, I never picked up the knack. I was a tomboy and loved to play sports. My idea of flirting was to say, "I bet I can beat you in a race to the end of the street," or, " I bet I can climb that tree faster than you." Yep, that gets them falling at your feet every time, if only from exhaustion.

By the beginning of August, I was splitting my time between the vacant lot, Katie, and highly-trained garbage surveillance of Pat, who, by the way, I was getting nowhere with. Mattie thought my crush was cute; my mother thought it was ridiculous. I'd really like to know how she found out.

One afternoon after saying hi to Pat, I came up the garage stairs into the kitchen and found my mother drunk, smoking, and playing solitaire at the kitchen table. As I reached into the cabinet to get a glass I heard her say behind me, "He doesn't even notice you; you're so skinny if you stuck your tongue out you'd look like a zipper."

"What?" I replied.

"You heard me," she said, as she placed the queen of spades on the king of hearts.

Funny the things you notice when someone finds a crack in your wall of defense and hurts you terribly. I just stared at the cigarette burns in the plastic floral tablecloth and wished for all the world that at that moment I could disappear into one of them. I didn't know how to respond; I felt rooted to the kitchen floor. I was conscious of a car horn honking somewhere on our street and someone hollering for Jane. Mom slapped a card down on the table and instinctively I reached up and rubbed my face. I started to feel very angry, an emotion that was not good to show in my mother's presence. I knew I had to get out of there before I said something I was going to regret and end up with a very sore face or backside. Slipping down the back stairs, I thought just once I would have liked to come back with a remark to hurt her as much as she hurt me; but I never did.

The next day another incident, like the one in May, happened to me and I forgot all about my mother's remark. My little brother Craig spent all his free time at the new building site in our neighborhood and as far away from Mom as he could get.

Late in the afternoon I set out for the construction site to find Craig. About two streets over from ours were six houses in various stages of construction. Wandering among the wood and sawdust, listening to the sounds of drills and saws, and talking to the construction crew made Craig very happy. He was such an inquisitive child. The construction workers patiently answered all his questions and made sure he was never in danger. After a couple of months they probably thought of him as their mascot. He was such a small child, I was always afraid one of the workers would step on him. He had turned seven in July and understood something was very wrong with Mom. I had coined a phrase the year before to explain her behavior to my siblings. "She's just sleepy," I would say. How much they really understood about Mom's behavior, I don't know. We never talked about the truth. I wanted to protect my brothers and sister. It was my job, along with Dad and Mattie's, to keep things as normal as possible. That's the way I saw it, anyway.

The temperature was finally starting to cool down after the blistering heat of the day. Heading for the newest section in our neighborhood where the houses had just been framed, I searched the first structure I came to. When I didn't find him there, I went on to the next. It was very quiet. All the workers had finished for the day and gone home to their families. Trying to avoid tripping over nails, screws, and sawed-off pieces of wood, I checked each of the six houses being framed on that street. Finally, walking toward the last structure, I heard voices.

The voices were coming toward me, and one of them said, "Okay, little buddy, that's all for today. I'm heading home."

I heard Craig say, "Then I'll see you tomorrow."

That's when they both noticed me standing in the doorframe.

"Well, well, who's this pretty little lady," said a man old enough to be my grandfather.

He was tall and wiry with small gold-rimmed glasses and a bald head. He had to have been the oldest construction worker I had ever seen.

"Craig," I said. "It's time for dinner."

"I know, you didn't have to come get me."

He was embarrassed and afraid he looked like a baby in front of the old man. To help him save face I told him I knew he was on his way home, but I just wanted to get a look at the new houses.

"Tell you what," the old man said. "Craig, you go on home and I'll give your sister a quick tour of the house."

I looked at him gratefully for playing along, and we headed into the frame. Big mistake. But how was I to know the old man wasn't as harmless as he looked?

He started with the bottom floor, showing me the living room, dining room, kitchen, and bedrooms. After the tour of that floor, I said it was late and I should go.

But he insisted I see the second floor saying, "It's the best part and you can't go before you see it."

Reluctantly, I followed him up the narrow wooden stairs for a tour of the bedrooms. When we got to the last bedroom, he motioned me over to the window. I'm sure bells were going off in my subconscious, but I couldn't hear them.

"The view out of this particular window is great – you really have to see it." He said enthusiastically.

As I stood by the window I could feel his breath on my neck, and his chest against my shoulder blade. I turned around abruptly, and he grabbed me by both shoulders and kissed me, hard. Remembering the window at my back, I leaned forward as I pushed him away from me. This wasn't school with the teacher in the next room. Scared and not knowing how he would react, I decided to pretend everything was okay.

"Hey, thanks for the tour, but I have to go home now before my Mom comes looking for me."

It was a good thing he didn't know my mother; otherwise, I probably would have been an unwilling participant in round two of "the old man kisses the preteen," or worse. But mentioning my mother seemed to give him pause, which was just enough time for me to get my shaking legs into gear and tear out of that house. I tripped on the last step, but grabbing the doorframe, saved myself from a nasty spill. I no longer cared about falling over construction debris. I was running flat-out for home. Arriving at my garage, I opened the backdoor to the car and climbed in. Rocking back and forth and crying, I tried to pull myself together before going up to dinner. Throwing my head back against the seat, I whispered, "God, please, enough is enough." Soon my crying hiccupped to a stop and I felt calm enough to go upstairs to the kitchen. When Mattie saw me she could tell something was wrong.

"What is it, honey?" she said putting her arm around me.

"Just a dead dog in the street, Mattie. It reminded me of Jeffrey."

I couldn't add my burdens to the ones she already carried with my mother. Another secret to add to the ever-increasing list. Lord, when will this ever end?

CHAPTER 11

Whoever Told You Life Would Be Fair, Lied

A couple of weeks passed and I forgot about the incident at the construction site. I had spent that morning at the vacant lot with Danny and the rest of the hoodlums. As I walked in the door for lunch, Mattie called from the kitchen, "Honey, your dad called, and he's coming to pick you up in an hour. Go and put some long pants on, and I'll have a sandwich for you after you've changed."

Changing into a pair of jeans, I wondered what was up and then all of a sudden I knew. He was taking me riding! "Yes," I said, as I jumped up and threw myself backwards onto my bed. Suddenly the grin left my face and the euphoria evaporated. Mom. She'd never let me go. She lived for destroying all my fun, especially with Dad. I jumped off the bed and ran into the kitchen.

"Mattie, where's Mom?" I asked anxiously.

"She left about an hour ago, but I don't know where she went." Mattie answered.

Oh, please God; don't let her come home until after I'm gone, I prayed silently, gazing toward the ceiling.

"Go on now, Sally, sit down and eat your peanut butter and jelly. Your father will be here soon."

I gobbled my sandwich, Fritos, and an apple in record time. Then I drained my milk so fast it left a huge milk mustache that cracked Mattie up. Wiping my face, she told me to go put on my tennis shoes. After tying them, I went and sat on the step by the front door – alternating between excitement and dread – depending, of course, on who arrived at the house first, my father or my mother. Bingo, I win. Driving up our street was my Dad's convertible.

I opened the front door and yelled, "Mattie, he's here! See you later!"

When he pulled into the driveway, I ran around to the passenger side and jumped in. He looked so strong and handsome in his riding clothes, the sun shining on his red hair. He smiled and squeezed my hand.

"Where are we going?" I asked eagerly.

"Well that's my secret," he replied, mischief in his voice.

I was so happy driving down the road with the convertible top down, the wind blowing my hair everywhere. This was so special, one-on-one bonding time with my dad was so rare; usually my siblings and I got one-on-one's only on our birthdays. But Dad knew how much I loved to be around horses, so he had decided to take me along that day to his polo practice. Because of his job, he spent a lot of time at the harness-racing track on the outskirts of Lexington. It was a perfect place for polo practice. As soon as we arrived, I slammed the car door and excitedly ran to the white, fenced-in arena to watch them practice. I wasn't even disappointed that we weren't going riding; just being with my dad was enough. Dad mounted the sorrel polo pony he had borrowed for this practice. He looked over at me and I waved. Trying not to lose my balance, I straddled the fence. Dad beckoned me to him. I was puzzled until he took his foot out of the stirrup. He always did that if I was to climb up and ride with him. I couldn't believe it – I was going to practice polo with him! What a wonderful afternoon! I probably only rode with my father for about fifteen minutes, but I wouldn't have traded those minutes for the same amount of time with Davey Jones of the Monkees, who was my current teen crush. I've seen only one polo match as an adult and couldn't help replacing one of the riders with the image of my dad and me racing around that arena smacking that white ball with a mallet.

Coming in the front door after the polo practice, Dad and I were met with a tirade from my mother. She wasn't drunk, but she was in a very foul temper. Knowing my Dad would be bringing me home, she didn't dare risk even one drink, much less a bottle. She drank vodka for a reason, to try to hide her drinking from my father. You weren't supposed to be able to smell vodka on your breath. What Mom didn't know is that she reeked of alcohol through the pores of her skin. It's a horrible smell, one I'll never forget. Mattie must have dressed Mom; she was wearing green Bermuda shorts with a crisply ironed white shirt. Her hair was combed and makeup applied correctly. What ruined the effect was her barely-suppressed rage. Bending down to the coffee table, she jabbed out her cigarette in the ash try and started in on Dad immediately. "You did not have the right to take Sally anywhere on a weekday. I have full custody and I did not give you permission to take her!"

Dad knew the conversion was going to turn real ugly, real fast, and told me to leave. I left and went outside to sit on the front step. Putting my hands over my ears, I tried not to hear how my dad was playing favorites with me and how that was definitely not allowed. If I went somewhere with him, the other kids went, too. I was not special; I was never going to be special. I pulled my legs up and buried my face in my knees. Why did she always spoil everything? I know you are not supposed to hate your mother, but at that moment I really couldn't help it – I hated her so much. Dad listened for about five minutes, told her she better not spank me, and left after hugging me good-bye.

I was halfway down the street with tears running down my face when I heard her call my name. At that moment I seriously thought about running away. All I had to do was put one foot in front of the other, keep walking, and never look back. But I thought about Dad, Mattie, and my siblings. I couldn't leave them.

"Sally, I am not going to call you again," my mother shrieked from three houses down. As I turned around and headed home, the image of a beach flashed into my mind with waves relentlessly pounding against the shore. I heaved a sigh and wiped my eyes.

Mattie was such a blessing that night.

"Your mama doesn't mean it, child. You know that, don't you?" she said.

I said I knew no such thing. She just held out her arms and gathered me to her big, soft bosom and rocked and sang to me for a very long time.

The Eleventh Summer

The next morning I woke up and forced a positive attitude. In about a week, I would be back in school and this nightmare summer with my mother would be over. The abuse might still be there, but not as often, since I would be in school eight hours out of the day. Plus, I was going to junior high. How cool was that? I left right after lunch to go to the vacant lot for the last time, although I didn't know it at the time. With my positive attitude came the courage to try something I had been too scared to do all summer. I had watched Danny and a couple of the other guys, on numerous occasions, climb the big oak tree with the swing in their hands. Once they got up high enough, they sat on the seat and swung down to the ground. Today I would do it. When I arrived at the lot, I noticed all ten of the teenagers were hanging out. I walked over to Tommy, the best tree climber, and asked him if he would help me climb the tree with the swing.

He contemplated me with his brown eyes then said, "Far out!" which meant "cool" back then.

We started to climb the tree. The branches were close enough together I could pull myself up from one to the other fairly easily. When we finally stopped on a very wide branch, I looked down and could not believe how high up we were. A robin chirping above my head startled me, and I clenched the branch above my head tighter. My fear made me swallow convulsively and say a quick prayer. The other teenagers looked like five-year-olds from up here. All nine faces were staring up at me with excitement. Tommy helped me mount the swing. My adrenaline was pumping and I was breathing hard from the exertion of climbing the tree.

Tommy asked if I was ready, and I whispered, "Oh, yeah."

Tommy was standing behind me on the branch, leaning back against another branch with the ropes in his hands.

"When I let go, you hold on real tight," he said.

I started to say okay, but never had the chance. He let go, and I fell at a rate of speed I couldn't have imagined. It was the scariest, most exhilarating thing I had ever done. It was a miracle I didn't sail off that swing and through the neighbor's picture window across the street.

When the swing came to a stop everyone clapped and my face turned red from embarrassment.

"Way to go, Sally," Danny beamed. "I never really thought you'd go through with it."

A girl named Cathy asked if I wanted to do it again.

"Probably not; once was enough."

She laughed and asked if I wanted to hold her new Yorkshire terrier puppy. I nodded yes and sat down on the ground with the puppy wiggling in my lap. I was still pretty shaky from the swing, and the ground is where I needed to be. Out of the corner of my eye I noticed three of the guys climbing the fence into the cornfields. I asked Cathy where they were going. She said they were going to get some corn so they could smoke the corn silk. I'd never heard of smoking corn silk. I would have to ask Mattie about that when I got home.

I decided it was time to head home, as I handed the puppy back to Cathy and started to brush the dirt off of my pedal pushers, all hell broke loose. A blue and white police car, with its sirens blaring, pulled up to the lot. The three boys who had gone into the cornfield were running toward the fence, slapping corn stalks out of their faces. Right behind, in hot pursuit, were two policemen. Teenagers were trying to escape in all directions, and I just stood there like an idiot, frozen in place. The police rounded everybody up and made us stand in a straight line. One of them got a pad of paper and started taking down everyone's names and addresses, asking if we'd been in the cornfield. I could hear the other kids giving false names and addresses, but I was so scared I gave my correct name and address. When they finished, they let us go and said they would be contacting our parents.

I was terrified. I knew I was going to jail, although I had no idea what for. I ran all the way home and stumbled through the front door, out of breath and crying.

Mom said, "What the hell is wrong with you?"

"I'm going to jail," I wailed and proceeded to tell her everything that happened.

When I finished, I waited for her to say I was a worthless, good-for-nothing brat who would never amount to anything. But to my complete and utter astonishment, she said she believed me when I said I hadn't done anything, and she would take care of it. She was also sober for a change. This was so rare and unbelievable, I knew something was up.

I found out later that evening what it was. Mom had a date. I couldn't remember the last time she had gone out with a man. Of course, I could not ask any questions like, "Who is he? Where did you meet him?"

The doorbell rang a couple of hours later and Mom appeared in her favorite red dress to answer the door. She reeked of perfume – I could smell it all the way back where I was hiding around the curve in the hallway. She opened the door and walked through, pulling it closed behind her. I didn't get one glimpse of the man she went out with. I watched through the bay window until the car lights disappeared down the street. Turning away from the window I headed down to the TV room to watch the last episode of the "Fugitive." It was one of Mattie's favorite shows, along with Dragnet. The fugitive might finally catch the one-armed man.

I'm an early riser (even on a Saturday), so the next morning I was up by seven. After the experience with the police, I felt a serious need to bond with my Barbie dolls. Knowing mom wouldn't be up for hours, I decided to risk playing on the couch for a little while. While I was sitting there changing Barbie's dress, a strange man with disheveled hair and wrinkled clothes came out of Mom's bedroom. He stumbled over to the couch and sat down beside me. He stank of booze and acted drunk. He wanted to know what I was doing, so I told him. It was fairly obvious if you ask me.

" You sure are pretty," he said leering at me.

Huge, clanging warning bells started going off in my head. Oh, no, not again.

"You spilled something on your shirt, sweetie," he said, leaning toward me.

That totally confused me, because I was sure he was going to try to kiss me like the old man at the construction site. I looked down and he put his hand on the imaginary stain. I jerked away and tried to stand up, but he grabbed my arm and started rubbing my chest with his other hand. Well, all I could think to do then was scream, so I did. It amazes me to this day that my mom made it out of a dead drunk sleep and into the living room in seconds. She saw what he was doing and immediately went ballistic. She was screaming, "Get your filthy hands off my daughter," while frantically looking around for a weapon.

Whoever Told You Life Would Be Fair, Lied

There was no need. The molester took off like a bat out of hell and never looked back. I looked at my mother when the door slammed and she just stared at me for a minute with tears running down her cheeks, then turned and wove her way back to her bedroom. I just sat there, staring at the coffee table and trying to absorb what had just happened, as my siblings slowly crept in asking what was wrong. Beginning to shiver, I told them there had been a bad man in the house, but Mom chased him away. Everything was fine. Yes, everything was always fine.

We saw my dad that afternoon, but I couldn't tell him what happened. He asked me why I was so quiet, so I told him I just hadn't slept well.

That night Mom shook me awake, instead of calling my name from the living room. She led me to the floral couch, and we both sat down. She looked so worn out and utterly exhausted, the lines on her face so numerous now. It struck me how very old she looked – not her age of thirty-eight, but much, much older. She very quietly told me she no longer wanted to live. Her words sent chills down my spine. Somehow this was different from the other suicide talks we had. How I wish I had known about the commitment papers and could have told her she was going into the hospital to get help. But I didn't know, so I just said what I always did. Everything would be all right. She just shook her head and said she was tired and wanted to go to heaven to rest.

"Heaven," she said, "is beautiful, with mansions and streets of gold."

I said, "I know, Mom, but it's not your time yet. You can't leave us."

She just gave me a wan smile and told me to go to bed.

A few days later I completely forgot that conversation. My mom telling me she was going to kill herself was the same as telling me to come to dinner; that's how often she talked about it. When something is repeated over and over a hundred times, you eventually become immune to the meaning behind the words. I wish I had taken her seriously and told my father.

CHAPTER 12

SUICIDE IS PAINLESS

As I walked through the front doors of Beaumont Junior High, I felt like I was turning a corner. I didn't exactly know what was around that corner, just that a change in the direction of my life would start here. That first day I just walked the hallways in awe, staring at everything. I had six classes with six different teachers. I thought that might be a difficult adjustment, but it wasn't really. What was an adjustment was carrying home more books than I had in the sixth grade. By Friday of that first week, I could actually feel my shoulders sloping forward.

The first day in English, the one open desk was next to a very cute guy. He was about my height, slim, with slightly wavy, light brown hair, and beautiful hazel eyes that any girl would envy.

"Hey," he said smiling at me as I slid sideways into the desk. "My name's Hank."

"Hey," I said back, dropping my English book and notebook on the desk. "My name's Sally."

The last bell rang and we both faced forward as class started.

If anyone had come up to me a few days later and mentioned Pat's name I would have said, "Pat, who?" I had a definite crush on Hank; and judging by the amount of teasing on his part, I believed that he liked me, too. By the end of the week I was on cloud nine; I had developed two new feelings I hadn't experienced before: hope and optimism. I didn't know it at the time, but both those feelings were about to evaporate. The next stop on my trauma train was looming into view.

Walking up to the front door after school on Friday, I was humming "Windy" by The Association and thinking about Hank. As I put my hand on the doorknob, I heard what sounded like an engine running. From the minute my hand touched the doorknob, my sixth sense took over and I felt that something wasn't quite right. The sound seemed to be coming from the back of the house, so I took my hand off the door handle and walked down the driveway to check it out. The closer I got to the garage entrance the more uneasy I felt. Rounding the corner of the house, I found the station wagon idling in the garage. The exhaust fumes made it hard to breathe and I started coughing. I couldn't figure out why my mother would have left the car running. She wasn't behind the steering wheel or anywhere that I could see in the garage. I walked up to the driver's side to turn off the car and through the window saw Mom slumped over in the front seat, her head against the armrest. My first thought was, " Oh, God, please don't let my mom be dead." I yelled for Mattie, not knowing Mom had given her the day off.

Fighting off panic, I yanked open the driver's door and Mom's head and shoulders flopped out like a limp rag. Grabbing her under her arms, I pulled as hard as I could to get her out of the car. Her shoes hit hard on the concrete floor and her left one came off as I dragged her to fresh air. I didn't know what to do – I'd never heard of CPR. I rolled her over on her side and pounded her on the back for what seemed like hours. Finally, she started to come around, moaning and moving her head a little bit. The fresh air had revived her and she started coughing. Kneeling beside her, I pushed the hair out of her eyes and shakily held her hand until she started breathing normally. My knees were stiff and popped as I stood up and walked over to the car to turn it off. It took three tries – my hand wouldn't hold still. I wondered how much time I had before my brothers and sister arrived from school. I had to get her to her bedroom; they couldn't see Mom like this. Mom struggled to sit up as I walked back to her. She was completely disoriented, not knowing who I was or where she was. I helped her to stand up and guided her to the steps. We slowly climbed the stairs to the kitchen, where she sat down heavily in a chair at the kitchen table. She was having trouble breathing again and asked me for a glass of water. Her eyes were watering and she was shaking badly. The smell of exhaust fumes was starting to permeate the kitchen from the open door to the basement, so I rose and shut it. After a few anxious minutes, her breathing evened out and she asked me to take her to her bedroom.

After I got her on the bed, she looked at me with complete exhaustion and said, "Thank you. God won't let you into heaven if you commit suicide. You go to hell instead."

She begged me repeatedly not to tell Dad and against my better judgment I promised I wouldn't. Then she told me to make sure I took care of my brothers and sister when they came home.

Leaving my mother's bedroom, I went to my bedroom, climbed under the covers, and let the shock set in. After the shaking stopped, I thought of all the times I emptied her vodka bottles so she couldn't drink. It had never worked. I thought of all the times I prayed to God to make her better and that hadn't worked. I thought of her almost killing Chip and the rest of us in the car. I thought about how she didn't want to live. I thought about the fact that no matter what she said, she would do this again. I felt such despair I thought I would drown in it. I got down on my knees and prayed a new prayer:

"Dear God, I don't want my mom to go to hell by trying to commit suicide again. She is so unhappy. Please come get her and take her to heaven so she can be happy again. Amen."

Later that evening as I stood at the grill flipping hamburgers, I thanked God that my siblings hadn't been home earlier and found Mom instead of me. I made sure they did their homework and had their baths before bed. I was pretty much cruising on autopilot by that time and so mentally exhausted that when I hit the bed, I went right to sleep.

The next day was Saturday. To my complete surprise, Mom woke up acting more normal than she had in a long time. Maybe what happened yesterday made Mom rethink the way she was living her life, and now she would get better. I breathed a sigh of relief and waited for Dad to pick up the four of us and take us to the farm.

It was a beautiful Indian summer day and I decided to put the nightmare of yesterday behind me in order to enjoy it. Dad picked us up in his yellow convertible with the top down. As he drove us out into the country, I tried to sneak up on the top of the back seat so I could really enjoy the wind in my face. Dad caught me with only half a cheek in position and told me if I were not back in that seat in two seconds he'd tan me good. I slid back down knowing he probably wouldn't make good on his threat, but best to not push it. He didn't like to spank us and usually did not have to. Using a stern voice and pointing his finger usually did the trick.

After Dad pulled the car to a stop outside his little house, we all jumped out, begging for carrots to feed the horses. One of my favorite black and white pictures in my house now is of the four of us standing on the fence feeding the horses. After the last carrot was nuzzled from our small hands we jumped down from the fence and headed in different directions. Walking beside Dad, I begged him to let me watch American Bandstand. He hated rock and roll and always said no, but maybe this time.

"Sorry, honey, you know I hate that music."

"But Dad, if you would just listen to it, I know you'd love it," I said earnestly as I walked backward in front of him.

"Go on and play now. I've got a little work to do," he said, smiling.

I really missed Adele. As I walked around the farm, memories would randomly come to mind. When I thought of us chasing the chickens, I laughed out loud. I became bored walking around by myself so I headed back to the cottage. I found my dad sitting on the couch reading and correcting some papers. I plopped down beside him and asked what he was doing.

"Editing an article for the magazine," he replied.

"What kind of article?" I wanted to know.

"About some of the top horse breeders."

I started to opened my mouth to ask what a breeder was, when he asked if I would get him a glass of water. His ploy worked and I forgot all about the question I was about to ask.

Later that afternoon Dad asked me to help with dinner. He was grilling barbequed chicken and asked me to put the Tater Tots in the oven. I helped put together a salad of lettuce, tomatoes, and cucumbers. He smiled at me as we worked together and told me what a good job

I was doing. After the table was set, we all sat down and Dad blessed the food. We all rubbed our stomachs when we were done, laughing at how silly we were.

Now was the hard part – going home to Mom and no Mattie. Driving back in the front seat this time, I looked over at Dad and wanted to ask him for the umpteenth time if we could live with him; but I knew it wouldn't do any good. The last time I had asked had been at the end of the school year when the thought of spending more time with my mother was making me sick to my stomach. He sat me down and tried to explain why we were with my mother. Before he had always said, "I'm sorry, honey, that's just not possible right now."

This time he said that the courts awarded custody to Mom and he didn't fight it because she really needed the four of us. I argued that she didn't act like she wanted us, but Dad just shook his head and said that she loved us even though she couldn't show it.

When we got home, both Dad and I could tell Mom had been hitting the vodka hard. My spirits sank, and my heart felt like it had been caught in a vise and squeezed. She had too much makeup on, the blush just accentuated her illness and made her look like a ghost. She was trying so hard to be coherent and fool Dad into thinking she was sober. I didn't know it at the time, but Mom was only a few weeks from being committed to the hospital to dry out. Dad had already found a house near his work so Mattie and the four of us could live with him. Hindsight is always 20/20. I think back, "if only" Dad and I had shared our secrets, things might have turned out differently. Dad took Mom in the kitchen, said something I couldn't hear, kissed us good-bye and left. The four of us looked out the bay window with tears in our eyes as he climbed into his car. He waved, and we waved back.

For the next two weeks, our lives went back to our regular dysfunctional routine. I really wasn't paying any attention to what was going on at home because Hank was all I could think about every minute of the day. We would laugh, whisper, and pass notes in English class. Our teacher was always telling us to stop talking and one day embarrassed us good. We were supposed to be diagramming sentences from the board. Suddenly, the whole class started laughing. Hank and I looked up. The teacher had put a sentence on the board that started with, "Hank and

Sally went...." We were mortified. Very clever of her. Hank and I could barely look at each other, much less talk. I felt such a strong bond of trust growing between Hank and me, a miracle, since trusting anyone was very hard for me. I hoped he would be in my life forever, but like many of the good things in my life, that friendship came to an end when I had to leave school two days after my birthday in October.

Because of Hank, I started going over to Katie's house more often for advice. I talked about Hank and she talked about Dave, the boy she liked.

One Wednesday, after school, I asked her advice while I sat on her bed watching her curl her eyelashes.

"Sally, you have to play hard to get. Don't follow him around or hang on his every word. Make him come looking for you," she said, lash-curler in hand as she looked at me in her mirror.

"I don't have to worry about that," I sighed. "We see each other only in English and occasionally in the hallways between classes."

"And why hasn't he called me?" I wondered out loud.

Exasperated, Katie explained, "Because most twelve-year-old boys are still very shy and not too sure how to talk to girls on the phone. Give him a little time. By the time he's fourteen, he'll call you," she said, giving me a wink.

"Very funny," I said, equally exasperated.

"Stop worrying, at least your guy likes you. Mine doesn't even know I exist."

Dave had yet to show any interest in Katie, but she was hard at work on a plan to change that.

Around the third week in September I was sitting at Katie's make-up table, while she patiently tried to show me how to apply mascara when her friend Sharon came by. Sharon became quite annoyed when she found me there.

"Sally, why don't you scoot on home so the grownups can talk," she said, as she smelled Katie's new perfume.

The ice cream truck chose that moment to drive by with its merry little tune wafting through the window. Before Sharon could open her mouth and make another remark, Katie gave her a warning look.

Suicide Is Painless

I was in seventh grade, Katie was in eighth, and Sharon was in ninth grade. Sharon thought I was too young to be hanging out with them and I probably was. I couldn't make any new friends at school for obvious reasons, so I dug my heels in whenever Sharon let me know she didn't want me around. That's how I knew about the party they were planning in Sharon's garage for some of the kids in the neighborhood on Saturday night. They didn't exactly invite me, but I figured they wouldn't throw me out if I showed up. I ran home that afternoon really excited about the party. What I didn't know was that my "trauma train" was about to derail the party in a way I never would have imagined.

CHAPTER 13

THE ANGEL WATCHING OVER ME TOOK MY MOM TO HEAVEN

Saturday dawned with barely a nip in the air, even though it was the last weekend in September. It was a beautiful autumn day. I was looking forward to seeing my dad and going to the party at Sharon's that night.

The first bit of bad news came when Dad called to say he couldn't pick us up. He had a deadline to meet and would be in his office most of the day. Great! That meant I had to keep an eye on my brothers and sister and make lunch and dinner.

When Mom woke up, things continued to go down hill. She was ticked that Dad wasn't coming and started raging about him shirking his responsibilities. She was really hung over, worse than usual.

"Out! I want every last one of you out of the house!" she yelled. "And don't you dare come home until lunchtime."

I didn't know it, but Mom would spend that whole morning drinking nonstop. We left the house and split up: Patty to her friend Jody's house, Craig to the construction site, Chip to who knows where, while I went to Katie's house. Mom was passed out and snoring on the couch when we got home. I checked for burning cigarettes and, finding none, went into the kitchen to fix lunch. When we finished, I told the kids to go play but make sure they were home by five for dinner.

Around three in the afternoon, I went to the kitchen to figure out what to fix for dinner. Opening the freezer I discovered there was no

The Eleventh Summer

meat, just some frozen brussel sprouts. No way was I cooking those. I opened the refrigerator next and looked for hot dogs. None. The last of the baloney had been used for lunch. I didn't mind cooking eggs for dinner, but there weren't any. Checking the cabinets next, I discovered to my dismay there literally wasn't anything to fix. Standing in the middle of the kitchen, with my hands on my hips, I remembered Mattie telling Mom she needed to go the grocery store a couple of days earlier. I was mad. It was bad enough to have to cook, but how was I going to get any food? Glancing around the kitchen, my eyes passed over the phone on the wall and then jerked back. I remembered Dad saying to call him if ever there was an emergency. I figured no food qualified as one. So, I gave him a call at his office and told him the problem; he said he would be right over with some food.

I didn't want to, but I knew I had to wake Mom before my dad got there. If I didn't, there would be hell to pay after he left. Once before I forgot to tell her when Dad was stopping by unexpectedly. He caught her in her pajamas in the middle of the day, smoking and drinking. There was a huge argument and Mom wore out my backside good for not telling her when Dad called. I had to get her up so she could put on her act and try to look presentable. Thinking of her smearing lipstick halfway across her cheek made me want to laugh, but I managed to suppress that urge fast. When I reluctantly went over to the couch and shook her shoulder to wake her up, she just rolled over. I shook harder. She finally rolled on to her back and blearily glared at me through the slits of her eyes.

"What the hell's wrong with you?" she said, sounding almost completely incoherent.

Her breath stank, a mixture of booze and sardines. This was going to be worse than I thought. She had to have been drinking straight all morning. Totally drunk.

"Dad's on his way over with some food," I said.

"What are you babbling about? He said he wasn't coming," she replied, trying to roll to a sitting position.

"We didn't have any food for dinner, so I called him," I explained.

"You called him? Did you say you called him?" she questioned.

The Angel Watching Over Me Took My Mom to Heaven

Pushing herself off the couch, she wove her way into the kitchen.

Grabbing her car keys off the counter, she declared, "Well I don't plan to be here when the bastard gets here."

I followed her drunken weaving down the garage stairs, frantically trying to think of some way to stop her from leaving. I was terrified. She was so drunk she could barely stand; I absolutely couldn't let her drive. She would kill herself or someone else. For the first time in my life, I switched roles with my mother. I had never commanded my mother before, but God must have given me the strength to do it that afternoon.

As she stepped off the bottom step and headed for the driver's door I yelled, "Mom, stop!"

I think the shock stopped in her tracks. All of the sudden I was mad, really mad.

Holding out my hand I said, "Mom give me those keys. Now! You're not driving anywhere."

I don't know for sure what it was, maybe the tone in my voice, but she handed me the keys without a fight. On a roll now, I told her in the same tone to go back upstairs and wait for Dad.

"All right," she said, defeated. I turned with the keys in my hand and headed back up the stairs.

I've replayed in my mind what happened next countless times, knowing, always knowing there was something I should have done differently. If I hadn't called my father about the food, if I hadn't awakened my mother, if I let her drive off in the car, if she had gone up the stairs first.

I was just about to put my foot on the top riser when I heard a crash. Whirling around, I saw my mom falling down the stairs. As she fell off the last step, she hit her head on the tire of the station wagon.

I cleared all the steps in two jumps, yelling, "Mom!" as I landed beside her.

Squatting, I put my arm around her back, and with my other arm pulled her upright.

"Oh, Mom, please be all right," I said, shaking and crying at the same time.

The Eleventh Summer

Her green eyes were dazed as she looked at me, but in a drunken slur she said she was fine. I helped her up, asking if she was sure she was all right, and she nodded yes. This time I made her walk up the stairs ahead of me, watching her every step. She was wobbly and hesitant, but made it to the top. I helped to support her weight with my shoulder as I led her to the living room and sat her on the couch. She told me to get her brush and lipstick. When I came back with the requested items, she said wearily, "You forgot the mirror."

I breathed a sigh of relief. She was drunk, but she was normal drunk. I didn't know it at the time, but those were to be the last words my mother ever spoke to me.

Dad got there within the hour and was not in the best mood. He wanted to know why Mom hadn't gone to the store. While they argued, I put the groceries away in the refrigerator and cabinets. Dad came into the kitchen and said he had a date that evening. He gave me the number for Harold, his assistant editor, if I needed to reach him. I knew things would only get worse the longer he stayed around, so I told him we would be fine. He gave me a kiss and left. I peeked into the living room and saw that Mom had laid down on the couch again, her back to me.

Around five p.m., my siblings showed up for dinner and I fed them grilled hot dogs, baked beans, and creamed corn. Mom was still passed out and knowing she wouldn't wake up until much later, I figured I had a couple of hours to go to the party before I had to put the kids to bed. I put Chip in charge and told them to stay in the house and watch TV. If he needed me, I would be at Sharon's house. Otherwise, I would be home about eight.

I headed to Sharon's around six in the evening. Her garage wasn't set up like ours; I had to elbow for room around the washer/dryer, clothes drying rack, old tires, and bicycles. I was surprised to find that Sharon and Katie were the only ones there.

"What are you doing here, Sally?" Katie asked.

Trying not to hurt my feelings she said, "I really don't think you should stick around."

"No, that's okay. I've decided to let her stay. I think she might enjoy learning something new." Sharon said as she smiled at me. That smile made me a bit suspicious.

The Angel Watching Over Me Took My Mom to Heaven

Within the hour, two guys showed up, Sharon's boyfriend, Bobby, with Dave in tow. What kind of party was this? I started feeling a tad bit uncomfortable. Sometime between the day they had planned the party and now, things had changed. When the boys pulled out the beer, my uneasy feeling ratcheted up a notch, but I knew it would be worse if I turned tail and ran. For the next hour I watched them consume a couple of beers each, which I declined. Without any warning, Bobby and Sharon started making out. I now knew she had let me stay around to humiliate me. Dave started to kiss Katie and I decided enough was enough and turned to go. As I reached the garage entrance, Chip appeared completely out of breath.

"What's wrong?" I asked apprehensively.

"It's Mom," he gasped, "something's wrong."

From the look of fear on his face, I knew this was not good. We raced home, my heart beating in my chest like a hammer the whole way.

I found Mom on the floral couch, lying on her back, as pale as skim milk and making funny sounds in her throat. There wasn't any 911 back then and I panicked, not knowing any emergency numbers. I told Chip to stay with Mom and raced to Katie's house. As soon as Mrs. Bennett opened the door I started yelling frantically that something was wrong with my mother. That's when I found out my well-kept secret was not so well kept. She told me there was nothing wrong with her.

I said, "Yes, there is!"

And she replied, "No, honey, there isn't. She's just passed out and will be fine when she sleeps it off."

I couldn't believe what she was saying to me; but I didn't have time to argue, so I raced off to find someone else to help.

Meanwhile, Patty had taken it upon herself to go to Jody's house for help. Running toward my house, I saw Patty and Jody's Dad coming up the street from the opposite direction. We arrived at the house at the same time, Patty and I breathing hard. Jody's dad took one look at Mom and asked where the phone was. While he called the rescue squad, I told Chip, Patty, and Craig that it would be best to go down to the TV room, so they wouldn't be in the way when the rescue workers got there. Chip looked at me with his big blue eyes, tears running down his cheeks, and said, "Sally, will Mom be alright?"

There was such fear in his eyes, Patty's and Craig's, too. Even though I was very scared myself, I honestly believed that when the rescue workers arrived everything would be fine, so that's what I told my siblings. They took one last look at their mother and went through the kitchen to the back stairs.

Thank God they obeyed and didn't have to watch Mom lying on the couch, her life slowly ebbing away. Jody's dad and I watched Mom helplessly while waiting for the EMTs. I wanted to smooth her hair away from her eyes, but I was afraid to touch her. Jody's dad was a big man and I was only as tall as his shoulder. He pulled me close and told me I was a very brave girl. I didn't feel brave, just powerless. As the agonizing minutes passed, Mom's breathing got shallower and shallower, then stopped altogether and I knew she was gone. I went still and numb. I didn't know I was in shock, my young brain trying to protect me from the inconceivable. Jody's dad didn't realize that I knew my mom was gone. In an effort to protect me, he sent me outside to wait for the rescue team.

After a blare of sirens, the rescue squad showed up and ran in the house. They were inside a long time, working on my mother and trying to bring her back. It seemed like the whole neighborhood showed up; everyone was milling around and whispering. Pat came over from next door and awkwardly patted my shoulder. Neighbors were talking to me, telling me everything was all right, but it felt like they were talking to me in a foreign language. Nothing made sense. It wasn't possible my mother could be dead just like a snap of my fingers.

I don't know how much time had gone by, when I felt Katie's mom's arms around me, leading me to her house. After about an hour or so, I remembered my brothers and sister. Panicking, I started yelling their names. Katie's mom ran in the bedroom and said it was all right – they were spending the night with other neighbors.

"What about my Dad?" I wailed.

She said they were still trying to locate him. I told her about the phone number for Dad's assistant. It was quite a while before my Dad was located and given the news. His assistant editor suggested Dad wait until morning to tell us about Mom – we were already pretty traumatized and probably asleep by then.

The Angel Watching Over Me Took My Mom to Heaven

Katie's mom sat with me for a while, tears running down her face. She told me how sorry she was not to have believed me. I just nodded, too full of pain and sorrow to talk. She finally left and I stared at the ceiling. I needed Mattie so badly; I needed her loving arms to hold me tight and take the pain away.

I couldn't sleep, and somewhere in the middle of the night I remembered my prayer for God to take Mom to heaven. At first I felt tremendous guilt. I had asked God to take Mom to heaven, and He did. But then I felt an inexplicable peace come over me. I believe it was God's way of letting me know she was with Him and no longer in pain. I looked up and whispered, "Mom, I love you."

CHAPTER 14

THE LAST GOODBYE

The next day Dad came early in the morning and collected me from Katie's house. I could tell he was trying very hard to keep his emotions in check as he kissed and hugged me. We picked up Chip, Patty, and Craig, and the looks on their faces broke my heart. They knew. No one had told them, but they knew. We walked slowly back to the house we had shared with Mom. Dad looked as exhausted as I felt. I didn't know he had spent half the night making arrangements for Mom's body and filling out paperwork. It suddenly occurred to me that Dad was as shocked as we were with Mom's death.

I put my arms around him and said, "I love you, Dad."

"Thank you, honey. I love you, too," he said gratefully.

Once we all were sitting on the love seats, (no one would sit on the floral couch) Dad explained that Mom had died from an aneurysm, caused by hitting her head on a hard object. My brothers and sister started crying. My sense of peace from the night before totally disappeared. I started crying and said it was my fault. I explained everything that had happened the day before, about Mom falling down the stairs. Dad pulled me in his arms and said it wasn't my fault. She was drunk and fell down the stairs. It was an accident. That was the first time he used the word "drunk." Mom's condition was always known, but not spoken of between us – a kind of pretending. If you don't talk about it, you don't have to deal with it. We didn't need to pretend anymore.

"Sally," Dad said, "your Mom has been hurting for a long time, and now she doesn't hurt anymore. She's at peace, in heaven."

Dad helped me pack clothes for the four of us and drove us out to the farm. Mr. and Mrs. Raible, the owners of the farm, had graciously offered to take us in until the funeral. I missed Mattie so much and I knew she was devastated by the death of my mother. Dad let me call her, and she said she loved me and would see me at the funeral.

My grandmother chartered a plane and flew in from Wisconsin on Tuesday, the day of the funeral. She hugged and fussed over the four of us. Because of the shock of my mother's death, the oddest things would come to mind. Looking at my grandmother, it really hit me that she didn't look a thing like my mother. She was tall and thin like me, with short gray hair and a fine-boned, aristocratic face.

Looking up at Grandma, I asked, "Who did Mom look like?"

She looked at me for a moment then said, "Well your mom took after her father. He had dark hair and olive skin."

"She got her green eyes from me, and then passed them on to you," she said, cupping my face and running her finger over my dark eyebrows, which were also a genetic gift from my mother.

"Why do you want to know?" She said, moving her finger up and smoothing the hair away from my brow.

"I don't really know why," I said pressing my tears into her neck.

Grandma helped us dress for the funeral. Around three we left with Dad and Grandma for the funeral home in Dad's convertible, and I wondered what would happen to the station wagon. The first person I saw was Mattie. She was wearing her "Sunday-go-to meeting" dark blue dress with a little blue hat, and a string of pearls around her neck. She was seated on one of the padded chairs before Mom's casket, crying. When she looked up and saw us, I saw two tears roll down her cheeks. I went over and hugged her and she held me so tight I never wanted to let go.

"My poor baby," she kept saying over and over.

I finally stepped aside and let Chip, Patty, and Craig get their hugs.

Grandma took us over to the open casket to say our good-byes to Mom. They hadn't dressed her in her favorite red dress, but in a dark blue suit she used to wear to church. Looking from her suit to her face, I noticed that it no longer appeared ravaged by alcohol and she really did look like she was at peace. All my tears had been used up, so I didn't cry. I said good-bye and kissed her.

After the brief service, Mattie put her arm around me and held me close. When I pulled away she looked at me with those warm brown eyes and said she told my Mom she would always take care of the four of us and love us just like her own babies. And she kept that promise until the day she died.

Dad, Grandma, Mattie, and the four of us went back to the house we had shared with Mom. Grandma stayed a few days and then went back to Wisconsin. We stayed on with Mattie in that house until we moved, a week or so later, to the house Dad had found for us. I had my twelfth birthday in the Pine Meadows house, and I remember that my friend Katie and lots of neighbors came. It just seemed so surreal to me. I remember getting lots of nightgowns. They felt so soft as I rubbed my fingers over them. I think Mattie told everyone to get me the same thing. She was so funny and so dear.

The day after my birthday, my mother's clothes and other personal items were packed up and removed. For the life of me I can't remember who took them. All I remember is an old prescription pad lying on her dresser, tossed there by one of the people doing the packing. I picked it up and took it to my bedroom. Written on the back were words in my Mom's handwriting. She wrote, *"What now my love, now that it's over, how can I live through another day?"* The rest of the words blurred and I couldn't read them through my tears. Setting the pad down I felt another rip in my already shredded heart. My mother had had no hopes, no dreams. I gripped the edge of the dresser and let the tears flow.

On Friday, the day before we moved, I said good-bye to Hank at school. I tried hard not to, but I cried anyway.

He hugged me awkwardly and said, "We'll keep in touch."

But, of course, I knew we wouldn't.

I put on my bravest smile and said, "I'm sure we will." Then I waved good-bye.

That night some of Mattie's family came by to see us. They all trooped into Mom's old bedroom, where Mattie was staying now. We all sat on Mom's king-sized bed and talked about anything and everything except Mom. Johnny, Mattie's grandson, had brought his baby son, David. I was in awe that Mattie was a great-grandmother. I asked her if she could believe how old she was now. She laughed, her brown eyes crinkling at the corners, and gave me a big hug, telling me she couldn't wait for some white grandchildren to hug.

On Saturday, the movers came and I wandered around the house for the last time. I went into each room, pausing for a moment in reflection while different scenes of that summer replayed in my mind. A few made me smile, some made me cry. I ended up in the living room with just that old floral couch left, up against the back wall. It wasn't going with us. Dad knew I didn't need a reminder of how Mom died, and Mattie's grandson was coming to get it. I don't know how long I had been staring at that couch when I felt my Dad's arm around me. I looked up and his blue eyes smiled at me.

"Are you ready to go, honey?" he asked.

Smiling back at him, I said, "Yes, Dad, I'm ready to go." As we pulled out of the driveway in my Dad's yellow convertible, I took one last look at the house, shut my eyes, and closed the book on my eleventh summer.

Epilogue

What enabled me to survive that summer? God, Dad, and Mattie gave me the emotional support and constant encouragement to deal with each crisis as it arose. I am eternally grateful to each of them.

My maturity and ability to be responsible came from my father. He wasn't just my father; he was my confidant and friend. He was always loving and supportive. He was so very encouraging as I struggled to put my memories on paper. As I write this I can't help tearing up because he passed from my life only recently. He went so fast I couldn't be with him, but I have three precious words from him I will always cherish. The day he died he said, "I love you." Nothing means more than that.

God was the only one I could tell my secrets to that summer. He knew everything, and although sometimes I wonder why He allowed those things to happen, I never blamed Him. In 1985, I developed a more personal relationship with Jesus, my Lord. Growing in Christ I now understand that God was always in charge, allowing me to go through those trials in order to make me stronger. Through the tragedies of the summer of '67, God gave me the ability to cope and stay the course in any situation I've encountered in the last forty years. But his most precious gift of all was Mattie. Dad didn't pick Mattie to care for me; God picked Mattie to love me. She loved me unconditionally through every aspect of my life until God took her home to Him.

The Eleventh Summer

Letter from Mattie to Sally in 1991.

April 6 — 1991.
1671. Corstigan St.

Dear Sally,

How are you an your family today? I am feeling good, Preketia is getting sweeter. I got one off the sweetest letter from my Son Chip yesterday. he told me his good news. I am so happy for him. he said he talk to you an m. Hackett about his good news, and he say he just had to shear it m. for I had a lot to do with what he did with his life. I told him, I made a promise to you all mother, that I would stay on, and do my best, to help take care of her children, and I did try. So when you all are happy, I am too. I am still praying for the other two, it was nice to talk to you the other week. I still haven't been able to reach mrs. Norkus, yet. It's not long before July, and it will be good to see your Smiling face again an mick and my grand daughters. So untill then, be sweet an pray for me.

122

Epilogue

My family Send love to all of
you.
 and much love from me
 always
 my daughter Sally.

 mama Mattie.

PS take
 all
 or mistake
 for love.

The Eleventh Summer

Epilogue

Mattie's death was actually harder on me than my father's. The day my family and I returned to the States from a military tour in Germany, in July of 1994, Mattie's daughter, Prudella, called me at my mother-in-law's house. She said Mattie was dying; and had only held on because she knew I would be back in July. She wanted to see me one more time before she let go. Somehow, through the shock, I told Prudella we would be right over. As my husband, Mike, hung up the phone for me, two warring emotions battled within me. There was the pain and sorrow of Mattie leaving me and the joy of how much she loved me. On the drive over, I told myself not to cry, but I knew I would. As we entered her bedroom, I couldn't believe this would be the last time I would see her. She was four months shy of her ninetieth birthday and her hair was almost completely white. Her smile was tired, but her brown eyes lit up when she saw me. She was so weak she couldn't lift her arms, so I gave her the hug she always gave me and told her no one could ever love her as much as I did. Taking her left hand I sat on her bed, with my family around me, and talked to her till she started to fall asleep.

Letting the tears fall, I whispered, "Mattie, I was so blessed to be loved by you."

With her eyes closed, she gave me the sweetest smile and nodded her head. I let go of her hand. Mike and my daughters, Alicia and Leah, said their good-byes. I turned to Prudella and gave her a big hug. She walked us to the door and said she would call when the time came. One week later, I received the call I had been dreading; Prudella said Mattie had passed on.

As I got into bed that night, it occurred to me that Mom and Mattie were rejoicing over their reunion in Heaven.

As I go to bed tonight I can see them welcoming Dad with open arms.

Resources

National Association for Children of Alcoholics
www.childrenofalcoholics.org
301-468-0985

Adult Children of Alcoholics
www.adultchildren.org
310-534-1815

Alcoholics Anonymous
www.alcoholics-anonymous.org/
212-647-1680

Al-Anon/Alateen
www.al-anon.alateen.org
1-888-425-2666

Federal Substance Abuse and Mental Health Service Administration
www.samhsa.gov
1-800-662-4357

To order additional copies of

THE ELEVENTH SUMMER

Have your credit card ready and call:

1-877-421-READ (7323)

or please visit our web site at
www.pleasantword.com

Also available at:
www.amazon.com
and
www.barnesandnoble.com

Printed in the United States
134617LV00005B/20/A